I0191347

Walking With The Lord; One Man's Journey

By
Cliff Montanye

Copyright © 2013 Cliff Montanye

All rights reserved. No part of this publication may be reproduced, stored in a retrieval system, or transmitted in any form or by any means, electronic, mechanical, photocopying, recording, or otherwise, without the prior written permission of the publisher.

Published by
Read The Bible Publishers

For discount prices on bulk orders contact
cliffcar@frontiernet.net

or write to
Read The Bible Publishers
288 Logtown Road
Port Jervis, NY 12771

or
Go to Amazon.com: books on the internet and type the title in the search engine to buy.

Speaking engagements are available.

Index

Part One: My early years

Part Two: Getting to Know the Lord

Part Three: Serving the Lord

Introduction

The writer of the book of Hebrews wrote that angels are ministering spirits sent from God to help us. Jesus said that signs and wonders would follow those who believed and preached the gospel. He also said that whatever we needed for ministry, if we went to the Father in prayer, He would give it to us.

As I look back on a life that started out as a scared, nervous, mixed up, skinny, high school drop-out, kid, I look back in awe at what God has done in my life as He eventually sent me to the mission field, used me in healing and evangelistic services, and put me in the prisons to preach.

God has sent angels to minister to me, He has revealed Himself in miraculous ways, and it has definitely been because of a life of prayer and an attempt to have a closer relationship with Him. This is my story, from high school drop-out to prison preacher.

The can of soda

"Through the Lord's mercy we are not consumed because His compassions fail not. They are new every morning. Great is Your faithfulness. The Lord is my portion, says my soul, therefore I hope in Him."
—Lamentations 3:22-24

When my wife, Carole, and I go on vacation to Virginia or Florida, I love to go to the shore and walk on the beaches. I used to walk as much as five miles up the beach, but I don't walk as far now that I'm older.

One day, a few years ago, we set up our chairs on the beach under the hot August sun in Chincoteague, Virginia. Then I started out as usual on my walk up the beach. As I walked along the open shore I could see about a half mile ahead of me and the sight of shells in the distance kept luring me further on.

After walking about two hours under the hot summer sun and picking up shells, I realized that I had walked three or four miles and I was very thirsty. I didn't have anything with me to drink and I knew by the way I felt that I couldn't make it back because of the exhaustion that was creeping up on me.

I love to talk with the Lord on these quiet walks with only the gentle sound of the sea in my ears. In Malachi 3:16 it is written that the Lord listens in on our conversations. I've learned to place my full trust in His word and I know that the Lord is with me wherever I go. I know that He hears me when I talk to Him. I know that He's listening. So, as always, I turned to the Lord for help. I prayed, "Lord, I'm tired and I'm thirsty and I can't make it back. I need your help." No sooner had I prayed this prayer and turned to go back when I looked down and there was a can of DR Pepper that had washed right up to my feet. The color on the can was badly faded from it bouncing around in the sea.

Sometime, somewhere, that can of soda fell off of a boat, as planned by God, and drifted, who knows how many miles or for how long, until it reached me at the exact time when I needed it. I picked up the can of soda that had been cooled by the sea water and drank it. When I got back to my wife, she asked if I wanted a drink. I said, "No, I'm good." Because I was. I was still refreshed from that cool soda. The Lord heard me and answered me on that day.

Just as those pretty shells kept luring me further on until I was weakened by the hot sun, life sometimes keeps luring us on until, before we realize it, we are weakened by its force. Just as God brought that refreshing can of soda to me when I needed it, He will bring refreshing rivers of living water to us when we call on Him.

But this experience was not something new to me. I have experienced miracles such as these for the past seventy years. From the time that I was born in 1943 until today in 2013. From the can of soda that washed up to my feet to the healing of the deaf as I prayed for people in India.

And that is what this book is all about. I've never written a book before but my hope is to tell you as best as I can how God has walked with me through the years and how He desires to walk with you if you will let Him.

Psalm 37:23 and 24 says that "The steps of a good man are ordered by the Lord, or are established by the Lord, and He delights in his way. Though he fall he shall not be utterly cast down; for the Lord upholds him with his right hand." In first Samuel 2:9 it says that "He will guard the feet of His saints." If we walk with God and pray and stay in His word He will establish us and bless us in all that we do. In Exodus 32:22 the Lord says "I will put you in the cleft of the rock and will cover you with My hand."

Yes, we will fall as the Psalmist wrote, but God's continual promises are for us and we will not be utterly cast down if we follow Him faithfully.

Part One:
My Early Years

The Prophecy

It all started when I was born in August of 1943. I was born with two crowns on my head, whereas most people have only one. The cartoon character, Dennis the Menace, had two crowns on his head and as a result he had what is called a rooster's tail.

My grandmother was a great woman of God who sought after Him all the time. It seemed that she was always sitting at her dining room table sharing the love of Jesus with someone. My grandparents loved the Lord dearly. My grandfather and uncle built the church that I grew up in. As my grandmother looked at the double crown on my head she prophesied that one day my feet would be planted on two continents. That prophesy was long forgotten until I took my first mission trip to West Africa in 1991 and eventually to India around 2002.

In 1991 I began taking short term mission trips to West Africa, ministering there in a financial ministry as well as a variety of other ministries that included preaching the gospel to the unsaved in India and holding healing services for the sick. As a result the people of both continents have been imbedded in my heart forever, thus fulfilling the prophecy that my feet would be planted on two continents. Although I've only been a lay preacher and had no financial support other than my wife's income, and my own, I've preached to two or three thousand people overseas and have seen many turn to Christ.

Azuza Street salvation

My grandmother and grandfather were Pentecostal and had been saved as the result of the Azuza Street Revival that took place in San Francisco, California, in 1906 and continued through 1915 or 1916. One of my great uncles had traveled to California at that time and was saved in that revival. He sent a letter to my grandparents regarding the revival and his salvation. I don't know what was in that letter but my grandfather couldn't read, so my grandmother read it to him as they stood in the front yard, and then she went into the house, leaving him standing there alone.

Whatever was in that letter caused both of them to fall under the power and the conviction of the Holy Spirit. My grandfather fell down on a tree stump in the front yard, not knowing what was happening to him, and cried out, "Where is Jeanette? Doesn't she know that I'm out here dying? "In the meanwhile my grandmother was inside the house, lying on the kitchen floor under the same power, not able to get up. They both received Christ that day and life was never the same for them after that. My grandfather had always smoked a pipe, but the next day, after he left for work, my aunt, who was a young girl at that time, noticed his pipe on the table and said "Papa forgot his pipe." He never smoked after that.

It was because of the influence of my grandparents and my mother that I eventually made the choice to follow Christ. I was raised in the little church that they built and grew up under their guidance until I was fourteen. It was at the age of fourteen that I became rebellious and stopped going to church. I never returned until I was twenty- four. Even though I was raised in that church and even though I was raised under the influence of a Christian family, nothing spiritual seemed to sink in. I was going my own way and at the age of fourteen I felt that I had had enough of church.

My father

When I was twenty years old my father had a terrible accident. He had a wood stove in his auction market and he always kept a small can of kerosene nearby and would put some on the wood before starting the fire. One day some men borrowed the can without him knowing it and used it for gasoline. When my father picked up the can it still had some gas in it and the ashes from his pipe, which was hanging from his shirt pocket, fell into the can. The can blew up in his face. My mother looked out the door of our house and saw him in flames, trying to put the fire out by rolling on the ground. She ran out and rolled him in a blanket and put the fire out, but by then he was burned over more than ninety percent of his body. The only parts of his body that weren't burned were his head and his feet. He lay in bed, in the hospital, suffering for three months before he died. I believe he was only forty-two years old at the time.

As all of the years of his life went by he never accepted Christ as his Savior, but during the last three months of his life in the hospital he turned to the Lord. It was the most beautiful testimony that anyone could imagine and people still remember it until this day. My father had a beautiful voice and loved to sing. As he lay on that bed, burnt from head to toe, he sang hymns of his Savior that no one thought he knew, hymns that he must have learned as a child. They echoed down the halls of the hospital for everyone to hear as he sang.

But my father was a harsh man all of his life. I remember the beatings and the verbal lashings that he gave me so many times. He always told me that I was worthless and no good. I never felt the touch of my father's love nor did I ever hear him say that he loved me, which is why I fell so much in love with Jesus when I met Him, because I needed the love of a father so badly.

The day before my father died he apologized to me and told me how he had been such a terrible father. I discovered later in my life that he believed that I wasn't his son and that my mother had an affair before I was born. The story was not true. It was a Devil's lie as Satan tried to destroy me and keep me from sharing the gospel.

That day, as my father lay on his death-bed, I lied and said, "No Pop, you weren't a bad father." I never cried at his funeral. Later in my life the Holy Spirit revealed my father's personal fears to me while I was praying and it helped me to forgive him, but it was many years after he passed away, and that's another story.

There were many times when I received a beating for going off fishing or for going off to play baseball with the neighborhood kids when I was supposed to be doing my chores. When I was ten years old my father had an auction market and a horseback riding stable. It became my job to clean the auction and take care of the horses.

But I loved to fish. I remember one time when I went off fishing and some kid yelled, "Here comes your father!" I was carrying twenty or thirty fish as I started running from him. The fish started getting heavy and slowed me down, so every now and then I would drop a few fish so I could run faster. By the time I had gotten into the woods to hide, he found me by following the trail of fish. Of course I got a pretty bad beating that day.

Right across the street from where our auction was there was a vacant lot where the neighborhood kids would play baseball. When I worked around the auction I could see them playing ball as I watched through the door. I was a pretty good hitter and usually scored home runs by hitting the ball out of the field. So, of course, being the kid that I was, before you knew it I was playing ball across the street and, as a result, received a beating.

For some reason my father felt that I should be working during any free time that I had, so I was usually punished if I went off to play. When I fed the horses or cleaned the stalls I was able to sneak off behind the barn where he couldn't see me. I would sit for hours, back there in the quiet, comfort of the horses, looking into the woods, watching the wildlife, and thinking.

I spent a lot of time alone thinking and pondering as a child and as a result it taught me how to spend time alone with God and ponder His Word, as an adult. It's amazing how something that seems so difficult in your life can become such a blessing later on.

My childhood

One day, when I was in second or third grade, my teacher asked the class to draw a picture of the house that each of us lived in. I drew a house with a flat roof that resembled a shoe box that was turned upside down. I drew two windows and a door and colored it black. When the teacher saw it she said, "Your house can't look like that!" The girl who was setting at the desk next to me said, "Yes, it does." My house was black because it had no siding and it was covered with black tar paper. It also had a flat roof. But I actually was more fortunate than some of the others. The house that we lived in at the time was small. It had a living room, a kitchen and a room to change in. We had no bathroom. We took a bath in a round galvanized tub and we had an outhouse in the backyard. A boy, who I knew, lived across town in a similar house except he didn't have running water. They had to wait for it to rain before they could take a bath.

When I was six years old I was sexually molested by

some teenage boys. I guess I was too afraid to tell anyone about it at the time because my mother never knew about it. I found out years later that she had suspected something was wrong and told the boys not to hang around me anymore. I apparently suppressed it at the time but I began to remember the scenes when I was in my early adult years. It still haunts me.

As I got older I developed all sorts of nervous habits. I blinked my eyes constantly, licked the ends of my fingers out of habit, and had nervous twitches. I was extremely timid and always lived in fear. We lived in a tough neighborhood and when some of the bullies realized that I had a nervous condition they started to beat me up when I walked home from school. One would hold me and the other punched me.

My father talked to their fathers and the school tried to help but nothing seemed to work, until one day another small skinny kid decided to help me. It turned out that he was tougher than any of them, in spite of his size, and they were afraid of him. One day after school he told me to get on his bike with him and then we waited. When the bullies came around and saw him they left and never bothered me again.

As a result of my childhood surroundings I became a rebellious teenager. When I was about thirteen years old I started playing dice and gambling with some other kids. I always lost so I began stealing items from my father's auction in order to have something to gamble with. I finally got caught and beaten by my father; so I stopped.

One Sunday night, when my parents weren't home, our pastor came to visit me. He told me how I was no good and that I was going to hell. Of course I already believed that I was no good so he didn't have to convince me. After all, this was what I was always told —and I believed it. So when he left the house that evening I decided never to go to church again, and I didn't, not until I received Christ at the age of twenty-four. But God had His hand on my life even though I kept falling deeper and deeper into sin. The irony is that the pastor who came to condemn me was later discovered to be molesting teenagers at the time, or so I'm told.

By the time I was in junior high I was a nervous wreck and scared out of my mind. There was a sandwich shop near the school and some of the kids would go there on their lunch break. One day when I went for lunch there was a group of teenagers standing around as I stepped up to the counter to order. I was so nervous with them around that when I ordered my sandwich I stuttered and stammered and the words came out all backwards. The guy behind the counter looked at me like I was from another planet. The kid standing next to me laughed and then interpreted what I wanted.

I was a skinny kid and I always wore long-sleeved shirts to cover up my skinny arms. I hated wearing gym shorts and tee shirts. One day, when the gym teacher took us out to run laps around the track I was so nervous and scared that instead of making the turn on the track I just kept running across the field. The coach caught up with me, hit me in the back of the head, and knocked me out. But no one seemed to care. No one bothered to find out what my problem was and, like many teenagers, I was probably too scared to talk to my parents about it.

When I was in fifth grade some of the boys in my class were as old as fifteen and sixteen so they dropped out of school. Some of them were in prison by the age of eighteen.

I dropped out of high school when I was sixteen years old. I had failed two classes during my grade school years and as a result I was two years behind the other kids. I wasn't a very good student, I was very withdrawn, and I was embarrassed to think that I would be graduating at the age of eighteen or nineteen.

When I was sixteen I had my first encounter with God's correction in my life. I had found some old army cigarettes from WW II in my fathers auction and went up to the pine grove behind our house to smoke one. As I lit one up I heard a rushing of wind high above me in the trees. Something huge and white had landed in the top of the tree that I was standing under and it was the flapping of its wings that I heard. At the time, I thought it was an angel who had come to warn me. I never smoked a cigarette again.

My first encounter with God's miracles

What I consider to be some of my first real miracles from God started when I was twenty years old. I was married shortly after my father died and my first wife, who was to leave me eventually, was eighteen. (I will explain this later.) We were married in December of 1963 and decided to take a trip to Florida with some money that was given to us as a wedding gift. We drove down to Florida and spent about two weeks there.

On the way back home it was dark as we approached Baltimore, Maryland and we ran into a snow storm. I could barely see where I was driving and somehow I got turned around and ended up driving in the southbound lane when I should have been going north. I didn't know how to get back onto the north side so I decided to cross over the median that was covered with snow. As I turned onto the median and drove a few feet, my old '52 Ford sank right down to the axle in the mud. I tried everything I could think of to get the car out. It was dark, we were alone in a strange place, and no one would stop to help. I cursed and I cried as I tried desperately to get the car out. I remember going across the highway and finding some old wood to stick under the tires, but it didn't help.

Finally, after I tried everything that I could, I fell to my knees in all of that wet mud and cold snow and prayed. No sooner did I pray when the biggest and whitest tractor trailer that I ever saw pulled up to a stop. In all of the mud and slush that tractor trailer was spotlessly white. The driver got out, put my wife in the cab where it was dry, hooked up a chain to my car, and pulled it out.

I couldn't get the car started after he pulled it out, so he started it and turned it around because it was now facing north in the south bound lane. He told me to get in the car and leave because there was a heavy fine for crossing the median. I've often wondered who that man was and where he came from when he pulled up in that big, white, spotlessly clean tractor trailer. Had the Lord sent an angel? He told me how to get into the northbound lane and he left.

As I drove away I looked into the rearview mirror and saw the flashing lights of the police and emergency vehicles coming to the scene. I knew that God had answered my prayers no matter how He had brought it about. Second Chronicles 7:14 says "If My people who are called by My name will humble themselves and pray and seek my face, and turn from their wicked ways, then I will hear from heaven."

I was not a Christian at the time and I had not yet turned from my wicked ways but the Lord heard and answered. Apparently I was called by His name and didn't realize it at the time. He told Jeremiah that He saw him when he was in his mother's womb. Paul wrote in Ephesians 1:4 that "He chose us in Him before the foundation of the world that we should be holy and without blame."

The miracle of the dime

The following year I turned twenty one and my wife was six months pregnant with our first child. I was out of work and couldn't find a job. We decided to go to Florida and stay with my aunt, who lived in Tampa at the time, while I looked for work there. Since I was familiar with working with horses because I had worked as a groom on a racetrack when I was eighteen, and I had experience with my father's horses as well, I decide to drive to Ocala, which was two hours north of Tampa, to see if I could find work with horses on one of the horse farms that were in that area.

I drove to the Ocala city limits with my wife and parked my car on the side of the road. The gas gauge read empty and I only had seven pennies in my pocket. Now, you might ask, how could that happen? How could I end up miles from home, somewhere in north Florida, with no money in my pockets other than seven cents, and no gas in my car? Why would I even take a trip to Ocala, knowing my financial situation and my wife's physical condition? And I would have to answer that I have no idea. I did a lot of crazy things back then and the only answer that I have, as I look back, is that I was young, made unwise decisions, and didn't let a thing bother me, as many young people do. This recklessness probably accounted, partly, to my total abandonment to faith in Jesus in future years after I was saved.

My wife and I got out of the car in the hot September sun, and decided to try to find someone who would let us use their phone to call home and have some money wired to us through Western Union.

We saw a gas station down the hill to our left and walked down to ask the attendant if we could use his phone for a collect call. He said no, and as we walked out of the station I noticed a phone booth on the side of the street. I walked over and stepped inside the booth and picked up the phone. Of course there was no dial tone because you needed a dime at that time to make a phone call.

We walked back up the hill, turned left on Main Street, and walked into town. After walking a few blocks we found a Western Union office. We went in and asked if we could use their phone to call collect and have some money wired to us. The woman behind the counter said no. She also told us that if the police found us there with no job and with my wife six months pregnant that they would lock me up for vagrancy. This thought hadn't occurred to us and it scared me. I think that the only thing my wife was thinking of was the hot sun beating down on us. I don't know why, but the situation didn't seem to bother her. She just followed my lead. We were just two kids out on an adventure.

We walked across the street so she could stand in the shade of the tall buildings that was cooling the sidewalk on that side. The temperature was close to a hundred degrees. She looked into one of the store windows and saw a penny bubble gum machine and asked if she could have some gum. I gave her our last seven cents and she went in and bought the gum. I don't know why it never occurred to me that I only needed three more cents to make a call.

As we stood there while she chewed her gum, I began to pray out of desperation. Now, remember, I had not yet given my heart to the Lord and I really knew nothing about prayer. But somehow I knew to pray and in some way I trusted God. While I was praying I heard a loud voice, like a shout, say "Go back to the phone booth!" First, I looked up and down the empty street, then I looked up at the apartments above me, and no one was in sight. I asked my wife, "Did you hear that?" and she replied, "Hear what?"

With that, I grabbed her hand and we walked as fast as she could go, back up the main street and down the hill to the phone booth. I stepped into the phone booth, picked up the phone and it was dead. There was no dial tone. " Of course there wasn't", I thought, "You need a dime to make a call." As I turned to go out the door, there, laying on the shelf, was a bright, shiny dime, reflecting the brilliant sunlight back up into my face. I hadn't seen it when I entered the phone booth. I made a collect call home to my mother, and she sent me some money so we could get back to New York State.

Somehow in God's own way, He spoke to me in an audible voice that no one else heard. I've heard many Christians say that God never speaks to us in an audible voice but they'll never convince me. As the song says, "I was there when it happened and I guess I ought to know." I had now seen two major miracles in my life and I had yet to receive Christ as my Savior. As a missionary once told me, about nine years later, "God has His sheepdogs on your trail."

I would not make the decision to follow Christ for three more years, all the time falling deeper into a sinful condition, mostly of cursing and swearing because I was so full of anger and frustration.

Was that an angel?

I got a job when we returned home but I soon lost it. Because of my lack of a good education and poor self-esteem I didn't hold a job down for very long back then. So that following winter, after our first son was born, I decided to leave my wife and son with my mother-in-law for a short while and head back to Florida to try to find work again, thinking that I would then send for them.

It was late at night when I got down to south Virginia and I saw a hitch hiker along the road. It was always my custom to help anyone who I saw in need so I stopped and picked him up. He got in the back seat of the car to lay down because he was tired. We got in a conversation and he began to ask questions about me. He asked me where I was going and why, and finally we got around to talking about my wife and son. He began to get me to think about them and miss them as he asked me more personal questions. He said, "You really love them don't you?"

By the time we got to South Carolina I decided to

turn around and go back home. He said that he would go back north with me. I thought that was strange since he wanted to go south originally. I took him back to Virginia and he got out right where I had picked him up. I never did see his face because it was dark. I only heard his voice as he rode in the back. I've often wondered if he was an angel who came to help me stay on the right track.

My conversion

Eventually I got a job working in a feed mill in Orange County. Orange County was well known for its dairy farms at that time and there was plenty of work in the feed mills for an uneducated man, although it didn't pay much. I worked there for three years and kept falling deeper into sin. The men that I worked with were rugged and rough. Lots of times there was cursing, fighting, drinking, and cheating on wives. I didn't drink at that time and I never cheated on my wife. I guess I was a good-looking young man because, at times, various women tried to seduce me while I was making feed deliveries, but the Lord had His hand on me and He kept me from giving in to them.

Because of my earlier up-bringing I still had some sort of mixed-up reverence for the Lord so I never used the Lord's name in vain. But I fought, I cursed, and I sat in on the filthy jokes that were told. One day I picked a fight with a man twice my size. I was a skinny guy and weighed one hundred and forty five pounds while he weighed about two hundred and thirty and stood about six feet and two inches tall. I teased and tormented that poor guy until he was like a raging bull. He chased me around the feed mill and once he caught me it didn't take him long to get me pinned to the floor. He then began to smash my head into the concrete and I can still feel it to this day when I think about it. I believe that he would have killed me if the other men hadn't pulled him off.

I remember when one man in that feed mill "got saved" as the men called it. Everyone was saying how John got religion and they would tease him about it. I didn't know that my turn was coming soon.

The work was hard and heavy but we were tough and crazy. We used to put a hundred pound bag of feed on our shoulder and run races. By the time that I was twenty four I had torn every muscle in my abdominal cavity. The muscle tissue surrounding my intestines were literally shredded and I had hernias everywhere. I had to wear a double hernia truss but there came a time when it no longer held my intestines in place. I had to have an operation.

During the winter of 1968 I went into the hospital for the hernia operation. It was supposed to be a two-day stay, but it lingered on for nine days because of the severity of my condition and complications that had set in. The doctor had to lift all of my intestines out of my abdominal cavity during the operation, place some kind of a mesh basket in the cavity, and then replace my intestines. He gave orders that I was not to get out of bed right away but the next day two nurses came to my room and got me out of bed, not knowing the doctor's orders. This action, on their part, caused complications and as a result I had to stay in the hospital longer than was normal.

Because of the ice storms that we had at that time, very few people were able to come to see me. I think I had two visitors during the entire stay. The first day after my operation my grandmother's pastor came to see me at her request. At that time I had no regard for pastors because of the experience that I had with my pastor when I was fourteen.

If someone were to tell me then that I would eventually preach the gospel to hundreds and even thousands before my life was over, I would never have believed them. I don't know what was said between me and that pastor on that day, but I remember mocking him and cursing at him. The man in the bed next to me joined in and as the pastor left the room and walked down the hall we continued shouting obscenities after him. Later, after I received Christ as my Savior, I went to his house to apologize and to give him my testimony, but he only opened the door about four inches and refused to see me. I never blamed him for that, after what I had done to him.

The day that he visited me, after he left the room, my roommate went home and I was left alone. The next morning when I woke up, I had a burning desire in my heart to read the Bible. I had never read the Bible in my life except when my mother made me go to Sunday School as a boy, and here I was, after all those years, craving to read it.

I called my Grandmother on the phone and asked her to have someone bring me the Old Testament. The fact that I thought the Old Testament was printed separately revealed my lack of knowledge of the Bible. She laughed and told me that they didn't print the Old Testament separately but she would send a Bible up to me. That day someone brought a Bible to me.

I've always had a habit of opening a book at the back, flipping through the pages until I reached the front, and then read the book. To me, at that time, the Bible was just another book.

I turned to the back of the Bible, to the Book of Revelation, and didn't get any further. I read about some things that were going to happen to this world, and even though I didn't understand them, I read Revelation from beginning to end and it scared me. I prayed, "Lord, I don't want these things to happen to me. I want you." I read Revelation 3:19 and 20 which said "As many as I love I rebuke and chasten, therefore be zealous and repent. Behold, I stand at the door and knock. If anyone hears My voice and opens the door, I will come in to him and dine with him and he with Me."

It was quite obvious that the Lord loved me because of the previous miracles that He did in my life. Little did I know that those miracles were all building blocks that would eventually cause me to place my full faith in Him. I'm here to tell you today that the Lord is willing to dine with you if you'll just take the time to let Him. I gave my heart over to the Lord that day, alone on the hospital bed, as the tears streamed down my face. I was completely changed from that moment on. The Holy Spirit entered my life and my vulgarity and cursing stopped instantly

I've always given credit for the day that I received Christ to my grandmother, whom I have always felt was praying for me although I know that there were others praying as well. But somehow I felt that her prayers were the ones responsible for the Holy Spirit pulling on my heart at that particular time. If you are a grandparent, or a parent, or a friend, or a relative of someone in need of salvation, don't give up praying for them. My mother prayed for years for my father's salvation and most likely for mine as well.

Revelation 8 says that an angel with a golden censor stands at the altar and he takes incense and mixes it with the prayers of all the saints —and you, if you are a Christian, are a saint. It then says that the sweet aroma of those prayers rises up to the throne before the Lord. Now listen to this. The fifth verse says that the censor is filled with fire from the altar, heavenly fire, and thrown to the earth and the earth trembles, shudders, and shakes because of your prayers. Saints, don't give up praying.

As I lay on that hospital bed, all that I could pray was, "Lord, I want You." The more that I prayed, the more the door of my heart opened for the Holy Spirit to come in, and the more He came in, the more I fell in love with my Lord and Savior. Many believe in Jesus as their Savior but not everyone allows Him to become Lord over all of their lives. Do you know the difference?

Jesus says that when you hear His voice and open the door of your heart to Him, that He will come in and dine with you, and you with Him. Can you imagine dining with Jesus in a fine restaurant, in a romantic setting, with the candle lights and the chandeliers? Jesus wants to have a love affair with you. He wants to romance you. He wants to dance with you through life. I have dined with Him and believe me there is nothing like it. When He comes in, all the way in, life is never the same. Many Christians live a troubled life of anxiety and confusion because they won't give it all, I mean every bit, to the Lord. I have always said that Satan cannot dine at the same table that Jesus dines at. Satan has to leave the area.

Part two: Getting to Know the Lord.

My baptism with the Holy Spirit

John the Baptist said, "I indeed baptize you with water but He will baptize you with the Holy Spirit." Mark 1:8

While I was recuperating from my operation I was pretty much confined to a bedroom on one floor of our three story house because I couldn't get around too easily. I had fallen deeply in love with Christ so I took the opportunity of confinement to worship Him every hour that I was awake.

Although I had been raised in a Pentecostal church I guess I never really paid much attention to the doctrine regarding the baptism in the Holy Spirit and so, when I became a Christian, I had no understanding of it. I was deeply in love and all I wanted to do was worship Him.

Then one day as I was lying in bed, worshiping Him in prayer, a strange feeling started to stir in the pit of my stomach. As I worshiped, the feeling kept rising up until it burst out of my mouth in the form of words that I was unfamiliar with and a glorious sensation flooded my entire being. It was like a river of pure joy was flowing out of me and I was praying in this strange language. Whenever I think back on it, the song "Joy unspeakable and full of glory" comes to my mind, because that's what it was. The experience was so wonderful that I have never been able to find the words to fully describe it.

Jesus said that "Out of your inner most being will

flow rivers of living water", in John 7:38. I believe that this verse has two interpretations. Jesus was saying that when we testify to others under the unction of the Holy Spirit, the rivers of living waters that He gives will flow from our hearts to them. I also know, from my own experience, that when I received the baptism of the Holy Spirit something that was beyond anything that is humanly possible to explain came from deep down within me on that day.

Although I received the baptism of the Holy Spirit that day, I never completely understood what the experience was until thirty years later when I attended a Bible study that was being held by an evangelist who was teaching about the baptism of the Holy Spirit.

I may not have understood what had happened to me but I knew that something had happened because after that experience you couldn't stop me from witnessing and telling people about Christ and how He changed my life. In Acts 1:8 Jesus said "You shall receive power when the Holy Spirit has come upon you and you shall be witnesses to Me," and I guess that's what happened to me on that day.

Baptized in a muddy fishing hole

Later that year, in late spring or early summer, I began to have a burning desire to be baptized with water. Again, just as with the baptism of the Holy Spirit, I had no formal teaching about being baptized in water. The Holy Spirit put the desire in me.

My mother had been going to a little Pentecostal church several miles away so I got the address of the pastor from her and drove to his house out in the country. I found his house and his wife was home, but she said, he was off fishing with a friend and she told me where to find him. I drove to the fishing hole where he was and told him my desire to be baptized. He and his friend took me, right then and there, down into that muddy fishing hole and baptized me. After that, I started taking my family to his church.

My first witnessing experience

After the Holy Spirit had entered my life it was like a rocket had taken off inside me. I couldn't stop witnessing and telling people about this wonderful Savior that I had discovered. I was a new Christian and knew very little about the Bible. As I look back on those days I realize that I had a lot of things mixed up. I had a lot to learn, but even so, I couldn't stop telling people about this magnificent salvation that I had experienced. Acts 1:8 says that "you will be witnesses to Me...to the ends of the earth." For me, the ends of the earth would eventually be India and West Africa.

I took a job as a fork lift operator after I recovered from my surgery. I could no longer lift heavy bags of feed at the feed mill. I had tried going back to work at the mill but I lasted only one day. In the course of that one day my experience with Christ became evident to everyone. I was a changed man and they all said that Cliff got religion. I couldn't stop telling them about Christ. The darkness of sin at that feed mill was too much and it overwhelmed me. Because of it I couldn't work at the mill any longer.

So I went to work in a factory. I learned how to operate a fork lift and my job was to supply the assembly lines with the materials that were needed. This job gave me the opportunity to meet a lot of the men who worked at the factory and to talk to them about the Lord. The men on the assembly line were mostly Hispanic and most of them could not speak English.

I found a way to witness to them on my lunch hour. Since I could not speak Spanish I would put two Bibles on the hood of my car, one in English, and one in Spanish and then I would open both Bibles to a passage that I wanted to share. I would find simple passages about salvation, draw the men to me, and then let them read the passages. They, in turn, would discuss the passages between themselves and try to communicate with me, asking questions as best they could.

One day I was invited by some friends to attend a

local Spanish church and to my surprise I found that some of the men that I had been witnessing to had started attending there. I have always ministered to Spanish speaking people at various times, even to this day.

Satan is a liar and a deceiver

There have been many times in my life when Satan tried to discourage me through people or events. One day, a few months after I was saved and received the baptism of the Holy Spirit, I was invited by some new Christian friends to go to an evangelistic service that their denomination was having.

The evangelist was speaking about the baptism of the Holy Spirit and inviting people to come up and be baptized. Of course I didn't realize at the time that I was already baptized by the Spirit. My friends coaxed me to go up front where this evangelist was praying over people. As I stood in front of him, he grabbed me by the head and started shouting commands to me, up close, in my ear. I couldn't understand him because he was shouting too loud in my ears. I said, "I can't understand what you're saying." He asked, "What did you say?"

As we stood on the platform in front of about three hundred people he asked again, this time with the microphone in his hand, "What did you say?" I repeated my previous statement, "Your yelling too loud. I can't understand what you're saying." He turned to the people and said, "This man has a demon," and walked away, leaving me alone on the platform facing everyone. I was crushed. He had just told three hundred people that I had a demon. I went back to my seat where my friends tried to comfort me.

Later, while at their house, they got in a circle and prayed for me. As they were praying, someone spoke in tongues and another interpreted. The interpretation was "My son, go to no man, I will teach you." When they finished praying I asked them if they knew that one of them had spoken in tongues and if they had heard the interpretation of the other. They all said no, they didn't hear anyone speak. I never went back to them again. I knew that both they and the evangelist were wrong. What the Lord was telling me was that I needed to lean on Him and not on human reasoning. In first Samuel 16:7 The Lord said that " The Lord does not see as man sees, for man looks at the outward appearance, but the Lord looks at the heart." The Lord was looking at my heart. Unfortunately, I never went back to another Pentecostal church for about thirty years because of my experience with them and with my pastor when I was a teenager.

I realize that this was really Satan who was trying to tear me down with another one of his lies. First Peter 5:8 says, "Your adversary, the devil, walks about like a roaring lion seeking whom he may devour." Jesus said that Satan "is a liar and the father of it," in John 8:44.

Not long after I was born the devil tried to stop me

from going any further in my life. When I was only a few months old I fell out of my crib and hit my head on the floor. The impact caused me to turn all blue. My father, who was not a Christian at the time, took me in his arms and cried out to the Lord to help me. My mother pleaded for my life before God and promised to dedicate my life to Him. As they prayed I started to breath properly and the color was restored to my body. No one knew the extent of my injury at that time.

In 2008 I was in a car accident. A teenage girl did not see my car approaching her and she turned into my lane while making a left turn. As a result she hit my car head on. She was driving a large suburban while I was in a small compact car. I broke my neck in that accident and the x-rays showed that I had broken the C1 and the C2 vertebrae. That is the worst part of the neck a person can break and many times results in death. When the doctors studied the x-rays they found that part of the vertebrae had not fully developed with the rest of my body and that I had broken my neck once before when I was an infant. This proved that Satan had tried to take my life as an infant and failed because of my parents' prayers at that time, and in 2008 he tried and failed again.

Our trust is in Jesus

Matthew 4:3-4 says "Now when the tempter came to (Jesus)... He answered and said, "It is written that man shall not live by bread alone but by every word that proceeds from the mouth of God".

There was another time, years later, when Satan tried to discourage me. The Lord was sending me on trips to West Africa, where my wife and I financed several mission projects with our income. I would go to West Africa on short-term mission trips, work on projects while there, and then come home to earn money to send back to Africa for more projects that needed financing. We gave most of our money to missions for several years, as the Lord led us. One day one of the elders of my church came to me and said that he worried about me because I was sending most of my money to missions and was not preparing for retirement. He suggested that I start putting money away for retirement and that I should go to the mission field after I retired.

I went home and read the sixth chapter of Matthew and how the Lord said that the Father knew my every need. I then went before Him and reminded Him of what He promised us if we would simply trust Him, not that He actually needed a reminder. I got down on my knees and buried my face in the carpet before Him and prayed, "Lord, this is Your promise to me and I determine to put my trust in You. You take care of my future and my retirement." I have never looked back with regret at the decision I made on that day.

Carole and I had often wondered what we would do when retirement came, how God would provide since we didn't save any money. But we never doubted. We always knew that He would provide, and He has, beyond our wildest expectations. As for that man, and others, who told me to wait for retirement before serving the Lord, well, they invested all their money in stocks and lost a lot of it when the economy dropped. Today they are sickly and unable to serve God in their retirement days. As for Carole and I, we're still serving Him. He has blessed us in every way.

Matthew 6:28 - 33 says "Why do you worry about clothing? Consider the lilies of the field, how they grow; they neither toil nor spin." So many people are spinning in circles in their toils of life. In verse 30 Jesus says we are not to worry as to what we should eat or drink or wear. In verse 32 and 33 He says that "Your heavenly Father knows that you need all these things. Seek first the Kingdom of God and His righteousness and all these things shall be added to you."

Jesus said that all of these things shall be added to your life. He knows what we need. Seek Him first, cry out to Him, and listen to what He says through His word. He simply desires that we put all of our trust in Him. "Trust in the Lord with all your heart and lean not on your own understanding. In all your ways acknowledge Him and He shall direct your paths," (Proverbs 3:5-6). Give everything in your life to Him and He will walk with you through all of your struggles. David wrote in Psalm 16:6 that "the lines have fallen to me in pleasant places," and you will find that the lines have fallen in pleasant places for you as well when you put your trust in Him.

If you're worrying about your future retirement today, or worrying about anything else for that matter, and it keeps you from serving the Lord, then you will

41

always worry. You can count on it. Always put the Lord first. Now is the time to trust God, not later.

In Luke 12:21 Jesus said, "The ground of a certain rich man yielded plentifully and he thought within himself, saying, 'what shall I do since I have no room to store my crops?' So he said, 'I will pull down my barns and build greater and there I will store all my crops and my goods and I will say to my soul, soul you have many goods laid up for many years; take your ease; eat, drink, and be merry.' But God said to him, 'Fool! This night your soul will be required of you; then whose will those things be which you have provided?' So is he who lays up treasure for himself and is not rich toward God."

The simplest miracles come from God

During the summer following my recovery from my operation I met three Spanish men who were educated men of God and owned farms in Puerto Rico. During the summer months they would leave their farms and families and come to Orange County as missionaries to minister to the migrant workers. Pine Island is a town near where I live that has very rich, black soil and is considered the onion capital of the world. Many migrant workers are employed there by the onion farmers. These three men would give their time and come to live and work with the migrant workers in order to share the gospel. I was still on disability from my hernia operation and not working, so I was able to drive them to various places where they could minister because they didn't have a car.

There was one occasion when I didn't have enough money for gas to go and pick them up. I felt bad about it, prayed, and then decided to go fishing down at the river that was across the field behind my house. As always, I took my Bible with me. While walking on the stones along the river bank and praying, I slipped and fell into the water, getting my Bible wet. I quickly got up out of the river and started drying it off. As I turned the pages I found two dollars that someone had tucked inside the Bible. Two dollars bought a lot of gas at that time so I was able to buy the gas and take the men to their destination. God knew that I would need that money and He had someone put it in the Bible. Falling in the river and getting the Bible wet was all a part of His plan so that I would find the money.

This was just another one of God's miracles in my Life. It was just another one of His ways of touching me, drawing me closer to Him and helping me learn how to trust Him more. Always look for God's small miracles in your life. Always give the glory to God for even the simplest things and praise Him for them. Never give credit to circumstances and chance. There are no coincidences with God.

The vision of the piece of paper

These three men visited my house often during the summer of 1967. They would come to dinner and then spend the evening in prayer with me. One of the men, Brother Angelo, ministered in the gift of prophecy. One day, as we were praying in the living room, he received a vision and appeared very disturbed as he looked at me. He said that he saw someone in the vision handing me a white piece of paper. He looked across the room at my wife, who had just entered, and then he turned to me and said that he couldn't bring himself to tell me what was written on it. He said that it was too difficult for him to tell me. Ten years later my first wife left me. That was what the piece of paper was all about. She never received Christ as her Savior, even to this day.

I need to say, right here, before I write any further, that she probably had a good reason to leave me. By the end of our fourteenth year of marriage, I was working long hours in order to support my family and other than to eat and sleep I was only home on Sundays, too tired to be a good companion. By 1978 I had stopped going to church. I had stopped reading my Bible and I had stopped praying. I had a lot of bills. I was worn out and tired, angry, and not much fun to be around. At the time that she left me I was still a high school drop-out and was having a difficult time trying to earn a satisfactory living to support my family.

The Bible

One thing that I did from the very beginning of my salvation was to take my Bible with me everywhere I went, whether it was on the seat of a truck that I was driving or on my desk. I loved to tell people about Christ.

My first Bible was a huge family Bible that you would set on a shelf in your house, mainly for display. It probably weighed about four pounds. I used to carry that Bible everywhere I went because I couldn't afford anything else and I imagine that it was quite a sight to see me walking around with it. I guess my grandmother became embarrassed when I went places with her and carried that big Bible, or she felt sorry for me. Either way, she eventually gave me a smaller Bible.

But gaining possession of that Bible was a miracle in itself. The summer before I received Christ we lived way out in the country on a back road that very few people traveled. One day a woman drove up to the house with the trunk of her car full of Bibles that she was selling. When she tried to sell us one we told her that we didn't have the money to buy it. She asked how much money we could afford. We told her that all we had was a jar full of pennies in the house. She said that she had a large family Bible that someone had bought on time payments and they couldn't make the payments any longer so she had to take the Bible back. We could have it for the jar full of pennies. So we bought the Bible and there it sat, waiting on the book shelf for me to read when I received Christ that following winter.

After my editors read the story of the Bible they asked me what happened to the Bible that my grandmother sent to me while I was in the hospital when I read the book of Revelation and received Christ? Maybe you're asking the same question. I've never thought about it until now and I honestly don't know. It's possible that I found the family Bible easier to understand because of the titles that were above the chapters or just by the way that it was printed. At any rate the whereabouts of the Bible that I read in the hospital seems to be destined to remain a mystery.

My first missionary experience

Proverbs chapter three says, "You will find favor and high esteem in the sight of God and man if you trust in the Lord with all of your heart and lean not on to your own understanding. In all your ways acknowledge Him and He shall direct your paths".

As I said, I carried my Bible everywhere I went, even to work, and told people about the Savior whom I had met. Even though I received criticism from some, I found favor in the sight of God and man as Proverbs says. In 1970 I took a job for a local newspaper distributer as a truck driver and eventually became the assistant foreman. The Lord caused me to find favor with the company and as a result I was able to take time off and go out and minister as God led me.

My first missionary trip took place when I was married to my first wife. One day, as I was reading the newspaper, I read an article about two women who were collecting clothing to distribute to coal miners in the West Virginia Appalachian belt who were having extreme financial difficulties at the time. As I read the article I thought that this would be a good way to help churches that were in that area to encourage the coal miners and take the gospel to them. I asked the Lord to let me take clothing and Bibles to the miners and their families. I always asked the Lord for permission before doing anything in ministry. I should add that at the time I started this ministry I had four children and was probably just as poor, if not poorer, than the ones who I intended to help.

If you want ministry, just ask the Lord. When Jesus said "ask and you will receive," He was originally speaking to His disciples and assuring them that The Heavenly Father would give them the tools for ministry if they just asked Him. Today it seems that we have taken those verses and have greedily applied them to our own personal needs. This is not what Christ meant when He said that all we had to do is ask. Paul wrote in Ephesians 4 that Christ gives the ministries to us that we may teach and encourage others.

After asking the Lord to let me take clothes and Bibles to Appalachia, I decided to contact the women whom I had read about in order to get some advice about how I could take various items to the coal miners. The women weren't Christians, so they didn't look at their work as a ministry. In fact they were in the middle of a lawsuit against each other, fighting a legal battle over ownership of their organization.

One of the women gave me some advice and told me

about a pastor who was putting a new roof on a church that was up a hollow in West Virginia at a place called Warrior Mines. They said that he had black lung disease that he gotten from working in the dusty coal mines and he was unable to work, but he was building a church and ministering to the people in his area.

A group of missionaries from some Pentecostal church had come through his area one time and met him. Apparently their church eventually ordained him and he was preaching the gospel. He was an extraordinary man. He couldn't read but somehow, by the power of the Holy Spirit, he had memorized the entire Bible and could preach from any passage in it. The Lord told me that this was the man that I should go to.

As I began sorting the donated clothing and packed it for the trip, the Holy Spirit impressed on me to sort and pack for three girls and a boy. I began separating various items according to ages and sizes of the children as the Lord led me. I had no idea that this man had four children. I also packed a football that someone had donated. When I got to my destination, I found the family just as the Holy Spirit had shown me to pack for. They were all the ages that I saw and the boy had been asking for a football. God had spoken to my heart and I responded. This was the first time anything like that had ever happened to me.

I made a few trips to West Virginia, and to Kentucky as well, over the next four years, from about 1969 and up until around 1974. I never knew exactly where I was going until I got there. Sometimes people just can't seem to accept the fact that the Lord simply showed me through visions as to what to do or where to go. They want to know details, but I can't give them the answer that they desire. I can only say that I had visions and I followed them, trusting the Lord.

On one trip I was collecting clothing but I had no destination in mind. I knew that when the time came the Lord would give me the place where He wanted me to go. As I prayed, the Lord showed me a brass musical instrument in a vision. I knew that this had something to do with my destination.

While collecting clothes at one of the churches that was helping me, I mentioned to one of the men there that the Lord hadn't told me where I was going as of yet. This man had no knowledge of my vision of the musical instrument. He told me about a missionary who came through the area a few months back and spoke briefly at his church. He said that this missionary had some sort of musical ministry in Kentucky, to the high schools near a place called Sassafras. I remembered the vision that the Lord gave me and now I knew where I was going. I had no idea where Sassafras was or what it was, but I was going there.

When I got to Sassafras, I found that it was just a small place out in the country and if you blinked your eyes you would pass through it without seeing it. All I had was a name of a town and a vision of a musical instrument. I had no idea where to go. I saw a man working in his yard on a corner and stopped to ask him if he knew of a missionary in the area who had a musical ministry. He pointed across the street and said "go up that hollow and you'll find his house on the right side on the other side of the creek." Now what was the chance of that happening? I found out later that if I had gone too far up the hollow I might have gotten shot at. There was a real-life Hatfield and McCoy fight going on. Two families were feuding up there, and if you were seen going into one house, there was a good chance the other family would perceive you as an enemy.

When I got to the missionary's house I had to park my car on the side of the road, walk across a long foot bridge over a stream, go up past a pile of coal in the yard (that would eventually be broken up by hand and used for fuel) to a modest house that sat on the side of a hill. As I'm writing this, I wonder, how did they get all that coal up there?

I introduced myself to the missionary, whose name, I found out, was Dick Bowers, and told him how the Lord had sent me to deliver clothes to that area. He and his wife said that they didn't know of anyone who needed the items but that I could stay with them a few days until I found a place to take them.

I stayed with them for about three days, learning about their ministry while I was there. Soon I had to go back home and had not yet found a place to leave the items that I had brought. They told me that I could leave everything in their garage and that they would find a place for it.

Before I had left New York for my trip my neighbor

brought me two new pairs of shoes to take. He said that he had sent away for them but he didn't like them. They were a special kind of shoe that could only be bought through a certain mail order catalogue. The ad in the catalogue read that if you bought one pair you would get one pair free. I remember that they were high cut leather shoes that were designed to go part way up the ankle and they had a strap with a buckle that went across the front of them.

As my neighbor handed the shoes to me, the Lord said to me in a flash of thought, as I saw something like a flash card going before my face, that they were for someone special. He said, or impressed on me —I don't know which, because it happened so fast —to put them behind the seat of my car. When the Lord speaks to me I sometimes see something like a flash card with a picture and with words, all combined, in one instant, but the words aren't in print form. Somehow I see the words as pictures. It's a very strange sensation that's difficult to explain.

As I was unloading the trailer at the home of the Bower's I remembered the shoes behind the seat of the car and wondered if they would fit this missionary. I took the shoes out of the car and walked across the footbridge and up to the house. When Dick came to the door, I asked him if he thought the shoes would fit and if he could use them. His eyes started watering up with tears as he asked me to come in and sit down. He went into the bedroom and when he returned he had an ad in his hand that he had cut out of a catalogue. There, in that ad, was a picture of exactly the same pair of shoes that I now held in my hands. Buy one pair, get one pair free, the ad read. He said that this was the only kind of shoes that he ever wore and he was just getting ready to order them.

I went back to the trailer to unpack the rest of the clothing and as I was unpacking I remembered two pairs of children's snowmobile outfits that someone had given me and I wondered if they would fit his son and daughter. I also came across several bags of baby clothes and wondered if the Bowers might know of someone who could use them as well. When I went back to the house and told them about the clothing that I had, Mrs. Bowers said that they were just looking at snowmobile suits the other day, and the Lord told her not to buy them because He was sending them to her. As for the baby clothes, she told me that she was three months pregnant.

After unloading the clothing and saying goodbye, I drove back to New York elated, as you might think. I was praising God and thanking Him all the way home. While driving up Interstate 81 I had the desire to take Bibles back on the next trip. I believe that it was the Lord who put that desire in me. I prayed, "Lord, give me two hundred new Bibles to take back to Kentucky."

Now remember, I didn't earn too much money at that time and I didn't have anything to buy those Bibles with. I was really quite poor. A day or two after I got back home I decide to visit the church where I had first learned of the missionary, thinking that maybe I might be able to give my testimony to someone there, since they had been instrumental in helping to find him.

When I got to the church, the parking lot was packed with cars. I don't remember what day it was, but I know that it wasn't on a Sunday because I would have been in my own church on that day. A missionary from India had come to speak to this large gathering on that particular day, which leads me to believe that the Lord had set all this up just for me. You have to watch carefully for God's miracles around you because sometimes they're only for you to see. Even though others may be involved, they may not see the miracle unfold because it's not for them.

One of the church leaders met me at the door and I told him of the miracles that happened on the mission trip. He said that they would give me the opportunity to give my testimony to the church for ten minutes before the missionary spoke. I gave my testimony and sat down. I could see that many people were moved by it. When the missionary got up, he told them that they should help me buy the Bibles that I wanted to take back to Kentucky. After the service people just walked over and stuffed my pockets with money and within a few weeks I was returning to Kentucky with a load of Bibles that I had bought from the American Bible Society.

This was the second trip that I made to Kentucky in a very short time, and it meant asking for more time off from work. Because I had found favor through the Lord with the company, I was allowed to go on the second trip in spite of the short notice. None of the people who I worked with were Christians but they respected my beliefs and what I was doing.

The miracle of the Bibles

I ordered two hundred hard-covered, black study Bibles from the American Bible Society. Why I chose to order two hundred and not more, I don't know, but as it turned out, it was the exact amount that I needed. It was just another one of God's interventions. I drove down to Kentucky to the Bowers' house to see it they knew of anyone who could use the Bibles but they weren't home. A neighbor told me that they were ministering at a summer camp for teenagers by the name of Scripture Memory Mountain Mission. I got the address from him and drove over to the camp to find the Bowers.

I found Dick and told him of the cargo that I had brought but he said that he didn't know of anyone who needed the Bibles. He suggested that we speak to the camp administrator and see if he knew of anyone who could use them. When we told the administrator about the Bibles, he said that he didn't know of anyone. He said the camp gave Bibles out as awards to the teenagers but they had a large supply of them in their storage room. He took me down to show them to me. The storage room was similar to a large kitchen with cabinets on both the top and bottom of the walls all around the perimeter of the room, but without the stove and sink.

I'll never forget that day, as he opened the cabinets

to show me the Bibles. He opened the first cabinet but there was nothing in it. He then proceeded to open all the cabinets, going from right to left until he came all the way around to the cabinet next to the first one that he had opened. As he opened the next, and the next, and the next, he said, "I don't understand it. We always order Bibles to be handed out as awards." There was not one Bible to be found. As he opened the last one, there on the shelf, was one Bible, exactly the same type of hard-covered, black Bible from the American Bible Society as I had on my truck. He said that this was the Bible they gave out every year.

I went out and got a case of Bibles and brought it back in. As I opened the case he saw the Bibles and asked, "Who sent you?" I said that Jesus had sent me but he refused to believe it. He said, "No, who sent you? Someone sent you." I couldn't convince him even though the miracle was right there before his eyes. As I carried the Bibles in I heard Dick Bowers trying to explain to him that this was the way the Lord worked in my life. Like I said, sometimes the miracles are only for you to see. Others may not see them or they may try to explain them away. When the miracles come to you keep them in your heart and hang onto them. The Lord will use them as stepping stones in your life to help build your faith.

Dick was the one who told me that God had His sheepdogs on my trail, and as I look back on my life I know that He did. How about you? Has God got His sheepdogs on your trail? Is He pulling on your heart, and if He is, how are you responding?

Prayer

Throughout my Christian life there were many times that I spent alone in prayer with the Lord agonizing over how to support my family because of my inability to properly provide for them. Jesus continually taught His disciples, and us, by His example, to pray. We see this example over and over again in the Scriptures as He would go off alone and pray for hours. If Jesus needed to pray, how much more do we need to? There was a time when I lived in an old run-down, farmhouse with hay fields behind it, when my children were small. I can remember going way out in those fields at night, getting alone with God and looking up at the stars while crying out to Him. The Lord has never failed me when I've turned to Him in prayer.

Prayer is essential in ministry or any other part of a Christian's life for that matter. James wrote , in James chapter five, that the fervent prayer of a righteous man avails much. He said that Elijah was a man with a nature like ours. He was just as human as we are. At times he was weak in the flesh and full of doubt, and yet look at all the wonderful things that happened during his life. Droughts came at his command and God even rained fire down from heaven. First Kings 17 says that he stood before God, meaning that he prayed continually. Elijah had a relationship with God and so can you.

I guarantee you that if things aren't happening in your Christian walk, that you aren't standing before

God in prayer for any length of time, because He is a God of miracles. One thing that you will find in this book is that everything that happened in my life was preceded by prayer, sometimes for hours, sometimes for weeks, and sometimes for years. I stay in His presence for hours at a time just worshiping Him and seeking His face until I get the answers. He always answers.

The house Carole and I now live in was built in 1837 and over the decades a few additions have been added which make it an excellent home to be able to get away from any disturbances in. Over the years I have designed quiet areas around our house, both inside and outside, where we can be alone with the Lord to pray, in order to get closer to Him and to hear His voice. I have built two secluded patios, and a garden pond with benches to relax on, where we can go off by ourselves to pray.

We have three or four quiet areas set aside in the house for prayer and reflection. I can honestly say that our home is a house of prayer. Most homes have TVs blaring away in the living room that drown out any chance of having a quiet time in the house with the Lord. This is a definite no-no if you have any desire to hear the Lord's voice. Not only does it create a disturbance but it also clutters the mind with unwanted thoughts.

There were times when I have prayed every day for a whole year before God answered me. One time it was before my first mission trip to West Africa, when I prayed for an entire year before going. As I traveled through the country I was told that I fitted in just as if I had been prepped for the mission there. There was another time when I was asked to go to India to preach. I prayed every day during the weeks before I left, asking the Lord what I should preach about when I got there. As I sat in prayer one hour before leaving for the airport, the Lord said preach on healing. When I arrived, a man was healed of a scorpion bite in the first service and people were healed in every service after that one. I'll write more about this later.

If you aren't in the habit of praying at least a couple of hours a day, I would encourage you to give it a try. Just start by telling the Lord how much you love Him and then pray with your Bible open in front of you. You'll be surprised at how the scripture will stand out and take on new meaning as The Holy Spirit speaks to your heart, and in turn you will find that you are developing a closer relationship with Christ as you begin to understand Him through His word. As that relationship grows, things will begin to happen in your life.

Keeping the high places

If you really want to serve God you have to allow any high places that are in you life to be torn down, through the power of the Holy Spirit. When I speak of high places I'm referring to the time when the Israelites offered sacrifices to other gods on altars that they had erected in the hills, while at the same time trying to follow the one true God. It can't be done.

The Lord says that He is a jealous God. He won't share His glory with any other god that we decide to follow.

When we decide to hang on to something that isn't of God, then we are keeping the high places that have been in our lives and we are no different than the Israelites of old. High places don't necessarily have to be some sort of sin that we hang onto, although it can be. They can be anything that we have a desire for that draws us away from God and keeps us from being fully committed to Him.

Take a look at King Asa in Second Chronicles, chapter 14 and 15. Asa did what was good and right in the eyes of the Lord. He removed the altars of the foreign gods and the high places of worship. He broke down the sacred pillars and cut down the wooden images. The chapter goes on to tell about the other things that this king did and how God blessed him, but in Second Chronicles 15:17 we read that King Asa still left a few high places of worship and, we also read, that when it came time for war, he called on the King of Syria and didn't rely on the Lord for help. It may seem like there are only a few small high places that are left in our lives and that they are harmless, but when it comes to decisions that need to be turned over to God we may find that our thoughts have become cloudy and we end up turning to the wrong source for help like Asa did. Asa kept a seemingly small sin in his life but it eventually led to his fall.

As a result, we read in Second Chronicles 16:9 that Asa would have wars throughout his life that would trouble Him. We read that in the end, when he died, they buried him in his own tomb, which he had made for himself. We need to be careful that we turn to the Lord and get rid of all the high places that might be hindering us, before we find that we've buried ourselves in a tomb of our own making. We don't want to live a life that will cause or allow any unnecessary wars in our lives.

I see so many Christians who are building altars in their lives that focus on other gods. Many Christians are bringing the world's views and the strife of the world into their homes and not turning to God in prayer, so the result is turmoil. If there are constant problems and turmoil that you don't understand the reason for, you may find that you've brought too much of the world into your home. Do what is right and tear down those high places that you are keeping and get rid of them. They only hinder your walk with the Lord and will keep you from being able to minister properly.

In chapter fifteen of Second Chronicles we're told of a prophecy that was given to King Asa: "The Lord is with you while you are with Him. If you seek Him, He will be found by you, but if you forsake Him, He will forsake you." Are you seeking Him and walking with Him? If you are, then He will be found by you. But, if you forsake Him, if you lean towards the world's standards, you will find that His presence is not with you and you will be asking yourself, where is God when I need Him? It's your choice.

Go into all the world

In Mark 16:15 Jesus says to "Go into all the world and preach the gospel." In Matthew 28:20 He says, "Lo, I am with you always," and in Mark 16:17, He says, "These signs will follow those who believe." The Father has given Jesus all authority and Jesus is passing it on to His church which is you and me. To sum it up, Jesus said to go into all the world and these signs will follow you as you preach. All of the miracles that I am writing about in this book are simply signs of the truth and promises of His word that have followed me through my life as I have attempted to share the gospel. There may have been times when they weren't visible to others but they were to me.

Paul wrote in Ephesians 4:11 & 12 that "Jesus, himself, gave some to be apostles, some prophets, some evangelists, and some pastors and teachers, for the equipping of the saints for the work of ministry." We're all involved, and Jesus is willing to give you a ministry if you'll just take it. John 14:12 & 13 says, "Most assuredly, I say to you, he who believes in Me, the works that I do he will do also, and greater works than these he will do, because I go to My Father, and whatever you ask in My name, that I will do, that the Father will be glorified in the Son.

He will give you a ministry and support it. Be careful not to try to start something on your own. Pray and be patient or you will become discouraged and fail. There will be times when people will come into your life and try to tell you what your ministry should be. Make sure that their opinion is of the Lord, and remember, God does send people along to give us a boost.

All one has to do is ask and Jesus will give you what you need in order to work in ministry and to glorify the Father. Remember that we are in the Son, Jesus Christ, and the Son's work is to glorify the Father. Jesus said that we are the light of the world. Remember the persistent woman, who Jesus spoke of, who went before the unfair judge. Because of her persistence he gave her what she asked for. So be persistent, prayerfully, and wait with patience for your answer.

If you want miracles for the sake of miracles or if you want the gifts of the Spirit for the sake of the gifts, you can forget it. It's not about the excitement of the moment. If that's what's on your mind then it won't happen. But if you love the Lord with all of your heart and you want to serve Him, then hang onto your hat because you're in for the ride of your life.

Paul wrote in First Corinthians 12:4 -10 that "There are diversities of gifts but the same Spirit. There are differences of ministries but the same Lord and there are diversities of activities but it is the same God who works all in all. But the manifestation of the Spirit is given to each one for the profit of all. To one is given the word of wisdom through the Spirit, to another the word of knowledge through the same Spirit, to another faith by the same Spirit, to another the gifts of healing by the same Spirit, to another the working of miracles, to another prophecy, to another the discerning of spirits, to another different kinds of tongues, to another the interpretation of tongues."

I have had the pleasure of ministering in every gift of the Spirit, except the gift of tongues for interpretation, at various times, as the Holy Spirit gave them to me for ministry. There are so many people who are sitting around and waiting for God's call when God's call is just setting there waiting for them to move. Jesus said to His disciples that the harvest is ready but the workers are few and I've found that to be so true as I minister in the prisons today. It's difficult to find people who will go into the prisons to minister to the men and women who are incarcerated because of their fear of the unknown and that's probably true for a lot of other ministries as well. People are simply afraid of the unknown and as a result they don't step out into the harvest.

The vision revealed

My life has not been without failures. Around 1974, ten years after I became a Christian, my life began to change. My church attendance stopped, my prayer life suffered drastically, and I was not walking as close to the Lord as I should have been. The financial burden of raising a family began to overwhelm me. I was working long hours, was tired all the time, and was becoming frustrated with my life. I slowly became a very angry person and was not much fun to be around.

My first wife began to talk about leaving me, and

one day, in 1977, I came home to find another man sitting at the kitchen table, visiting with her. I simply went out to the back yard and waited for their visit to be over. She began seeing him during that year and in 1978 our marriage ended. It was devastating. The vision that Brother Angelo had several years earlier of someone handing me a piece of paper came true. The sheet of paper that he had seen were the divorce papers. I had never known what his vision meant but now I understood why it hurt him so much at the time. He knew that eventually I was going to go through a divorce. In Hebrew the word divorce means a cutting or to cut apart. Our family had now been fiercely cut apart. I had loved my wife with all of my heart, but my anxiety and anger had caused us to separate. I had pushed her love away from me. I begged her to reconsider, but it was too late. She took two of our five children and the other three stayed with me, although two more went to live with her a few years later while my youngest son remained with me.

Marred in the potters hands

I never believed that a marriage should end in divorce and I still don't. It was never God's plan for two people to be torn apart with so much pain. I believed that there was no place in God's plan for a divorced person and that it was an unpardonable sin. I believed that God had turned His back on me completely because of my sin and that there was no forgiveness for me, but that was the devil's lie. I was very, very, wrong and had a poor understanding of

God's love for me.

I've heard so many preachers say that when we make serious, sinful mistakes, God has to change His plan for us and that we can only expect second best in our lives. I'm here to tell you right now that it isn't true. First John 1:9 says, "If we confess our sins, He is faithful and just to forgive us our sins and to cleanse us from all unrighteousness". In chapter 2:1 it says, "If anyone sins we have an advocate with the Father, Jesus Christ the righteous". Plans get changed in our lives but we never have to worry about having second best because of God's judgment on us.

I'm reminded of God's command to Jeremiah that's recorded in Jeremiah, chapter 18. "The Lord said, 'Go down to the potter's house and there I will cause you to hear My words.' Jeremiah went down to the potter's house and the potter was making something on the wheel with clay. The vessel of clay that the potter was making was marred in the potters hand," just as we are at times. "So he made it again, he reshaped it as it seemed good to the potter to make. Then the word of the Lord came to Jeremiah and said, 'Oh house of Israel, can I not do with you as this potter has done? As the clay is in the potter's hands, so are you in My hand." I would like to suggest that if you feel that you have been marred in the Potter's hands, that you visit a potter's house at some time and watch him work for a while.

One day I personally had the chance to go to a potter's house and I was surprised at what I saw. It was not what I had expected to see at all as I watched the potter make vase after vase. Suddenly one dropped from his hand into a shapeless pile of clay on the wheel but the potter never stopped working. The wheel kept spinning as he brought that pile of marred clay back up and formed it, not into a vessel like the others that he was making, but instead, it turned into a beautiful creation all it's own. The potter then picked it up and placed it on a separate shelf. It was there that I saw all the vessels that had been marred in his hands previously, all of them setting on the shelf in their own individual, magnificent beauty. It was only then that I really understood the story of Jeremiah and the potter's house. We may become marred at times, but God knows how to take our lives into His hands and how to shape us into something much better than what we were.

I realized that God had not turned his back on me at all. Instead, he was there ready to forgive me and to heal my pain when I turned to Him. He was about to bring circumstances into my life that would change me forever. Don't ever believe that God has turned His back on you because of the negative circumstances that you may be in at the time. It's we who turn our backs on Him. He will never leave us. He's always there, waiting for us to turn back to Him.

Misunderstanding God and His word

At the time of my divorce I believed that God wanted nothing to do with me and, as a result of that belief, I back-slid and fell deep into sin. I had a lot to learn about God's grace. I started drinking and smoking pot in order to drown out my sorrow. My family was broken up, I lost my wife, and I believed that I had lost the Lord. I was either drunk on alcohol or high on drugs every day, around the clock, for almost all of 1978. When I talked about it to my children years later, I found out that they were never aware of my condition. I was always trying to find consolation with other women in order to rid myself of my sorrow, but they in turn were hurting just as much as I was.

Every night I would lie on my bed, drunk, crying out for the Lord to help me and at the same time believing that He did not want anything to do with me. As a result I felt that He would not come near me. The confusion was tearing me apart.

In spite of my drunkenness and the sin that I had fallen into, God still kept His protective hand on my life. One afternoon, while I was drunk, my mother came to visit me as I was preparing dinner for the kids. I had been cooking pork chops in the oven at 350 degrees for about an hour. As she sat at the kitchen table watching me, I opened the oven door and reached in with my bare hands to grab the hot, greasy, bubbling pan of pork chops. Before she could say a word, I picked the tray up and placed it on the stove top without thinking about the heat. I had no pain and there were no burn marks on my hands. After I set the pan down I realized what had happened.

My sorrow grew deeper and deeper until finally on New Year's Eve of 1979 I decided to take my life. I swallowed several bottles of medicine that I had gotten, besides drinking a bottle of liquor and smoking some pot. Later, after the doctors examined me, I found out that I had a complete nervous breakdown at the same time.

I laid down to die that evening and five days later I regained consciousness in a rehabilitation center at the local hospital. The other patients told me that I had been walking around and talking as if everything was normal during those five days but I was totally unaware of my surroundings. The last thing that I remembered seeing was the ball dropping in Times Square as I watched TV on New Years Eve. The doctors told me that I took enough drugs to kill five men but there were a few antibiotics mixed in with the medicine and that was what kept me alive.

My mother was the one who took me to the hospital and she asked the doctor if the drugs had caused any brain damage. He told her that I was capable of doing anything that I set my mind to do, and I have proved him to be right over the years. It was not God's time for me to die. The Lord had many things for me to do and many people for me to reach. I was in the hospital for three months while getting my life back together, and while I was there I asked for my Bible and my Bible Concordance. God had stopped me on my downhill slide and gotten my attention. Now, once again, I began studying His word.

The agony of Gethsemane

One day as I was crying out to God and praying strenuously, my face became hot and sweaty from the intensity of the prayer. I went into the bathroom to splash some cold water on my face and when I looked at my reflection in the mirror I saw drops of blood coming from the pores on my forehead because I had been praying so hard. When I saw the drops of blood it reminded me of the drops of blood that fell from Jesus' forehead while He prayed in agony at Gethsemane, as it is recorded in Luke 22:44. I thought of all that He had gone through in order to obtain forgiveness for me, and I realized at that moment that He would forgive me no matter what I was or what I did.

When John wrote in First John chapter one that Jesus is faithful and just to forgive us our sins he was reminding believers that we all have sin in us and that we all make mistakes at some time or another and that we are not to get discouraged when we fall because He is always there to pick us up. The psalmist reminds us, in Psalm 37, that when a good man falls he shall not utterly be cast down because the Lord will hold him up with His hand. Notice that it says that "he shall not be utterly cast down," which indicates that we may fall at times. If you ever find yourself in the position of falling always remember that He's there for you. David wrote in Psalm 37:25, "I have been young and now am old, yet I have not seen the righteous forsaken nor his descendants begging bread." As I realized the extent of God's forgiveness, I began, once again, to seek God as I did in the past.

Climbing back up

In Second Chronicles 20:3, 9 and 12 it's recorded that when the enemy came against Jehoshaphat, that "he feared and set himself to seek the Lord and proclaimed a fast throughout all of Judah." He prayed that "If disaster comes upon us we will stand in Your presence and cry out to you and you will hear and save." Just as with Jehoshaphat, when disaster comes against us we need to stand before God with as much strength as possible, and cry out to Him until He answers. Our eyes must always be focused on Him. Sometimes it's difficult and it seems almost impossible. Psalm 91:7 says that a thousand may fall at your right hand but destruction will not come near you when your eyes are on the Lord. If you're in a bad situation just stay focused on Him and He will get you out of it.

One day during the three months that I was in the hospital recuperating, my back began to hurt me severely. Because the problem persisted, someone brought a chiropractor to me, who turned out to be a Christian. He was an elder in the Christian and Missionary Alliance Church and eventually became a friend. Because of him I began attending his church when I was released from the hospital, since I had no church of my own at the time. I remained in that church for twenty-one years until the need to go into a new ministry moved me on.

While at that church I was appointed as one of the trustees for the church grounds, then I was appointed as a deacon, and later, as I grew in the Lord, I was appointed as the local Alliance Men's President for a period of six years. You were not allowed to be an elder in the C&MA at the time, if you were divorced, so later I moved on in order to get into other ministries. It was in the C&MA church that I learned all about the missionary field, and during my time there I traveled back and forth to the mission field in West Africa for about ten years. After leaving this church I went on to other ministries such as local TV ministry, street ministry, prison ministry, healing ministry, evangelistic ministry, and more, eventually traveling back and forth to India for five years. Many miracles took place in my life during those times, which I'll write about later in this book.

At the time that I was in the hospital recuperating from my breakdown I was thirty-five years old. I had dropped out of high school at the age of sixteen but had earned a high school equivalency diploma when I was thirty and now, while in the hospital, I decided that it was time to go to college and prepare for ministry. A social worker helped me to prepare for college since I was eligible for rehabilitation under the state law. If I hadn't had the breakdown, it's possible that I would never have been able to go to college due to a of a lack of finances.

Although the state didn't pay for my college it helped me to get my education up to college level and it got me going in the right direction in order to obtain government grants. It was extremely embarrassing at first because they started me at the most basic level of education. I was placed in a first grade level math and reading class where I was taught that one plus one equals two and they used the first grade book "See Spot Run." But it gave me a solid foundation as a base to further my education on and I was always grateful for that.

It took me almost four years to fully recuperate from my breakdown. During those years I went to therapy while I slowly got off the medication that I was taking for depression. After going through the basic courses I went to college while working part time and raising three children. I was living on an income from part time work, food stamps , and grants. At first my children and I lived in a small garage that my mother had renovated for us and later we moved into a small apartment that she rented out to tenants for extra income. I had to sell the house that my ex-wife and I had bought because she wanted her share of the money from it. I really wasn't capable of maintaining it anyway because I was still trying to regain stability at the time.

God sent Jeff a toy box

I didn't have much money and I couldn't afford to buy all the things that my children would like to have had as I was recuperating and going to college. One day my youngest son, Jeff, who was about nine or ten years old at the time, came to me and told me that there were some toys that he would like to have and he described them to me. He said that he would like to have a wooden toy box that looked like a foot locker, with horses and cows and cowboys and Indians inscribed on it. He told me of the games and all the other toys that he would like. As he told me of his desires it broke my heart because I knew that I couldn't afford any of them.

Jeff had come to love the Lord very much at the age of eight or nine, and still does. He would always tell the other kids at school about Jesus. So I said, "Let's pray and ask the Lord for these things," never expecting the miracle that would soon take place in our lives and would be a reminder to me, to this day, as to how God listens in on our conversations.

We knelt down and Jeff prayed for all the things that he had on his list including many household items that I needed. Now there was a patch of woods near us where the kids would play. They had trails winding through them where the kids rode their bikes and motorcycles, and sometimes people would illegally dump their unwanted items there.

A few days after Jeff had prayed, he came running down to the house, all out of breath and excited, yelling for me to come with him to see what he had found. There in the woods, someone had dumped every single item that Jeff had prayed for, exactly as he had described them. There was the toy box, with cowboys lassoing cows, and Indians riding horses, inscribed on it, and all the games that he wanted along with the other toys that he had prayed for, plus lamps for the apartment, towels and wash cloths along with other household items that we needed, all brand-new with price tags still on some of them and all packed in boxes that were stacked in a neat pile. We loaded up the trunk of my car and took them home.

It was as if the person who was responsible for leaving these items had been sitting in the next room while we were talking, listening to every word, and of course He was. In Malachi 3:16 and 17 it is written that "Those who feared the Lord spoke to one another and the Lord listened and heard them. So a book of remembrance was written before Him for those who fear the Lord and who meditate on His name. 'They shall be Mine,' says the Lord of hosts, 'on the day that I make them my jewels, and I will spare them.'" The only thing that the Lord desires of you, today, is your faith and trust in Him, with a childlike expectation. Isn't it time to stop making our lives so complicated and time to turn everything over to Him?

In Matthew 19:14 Jesus said, "Let the little children come to Me and do not forbid them, for as such is the kingdom of Heaven." And in Matthew 18:3 He said that "Unless you are converted and become as little children you will by no means enter the kingdom of Heaven." Jeff had gone to Jesus, and standing before the throne of grace, he entered into the kingdom of Heaven through prayer.

He was just a young boy who trusted the Lord and took Him at His word. He had never read all the books that so many people seem to think one has to read in order to understand how to get close to God. He just prayed a simple prayer and believed as only a child could believe, and God didn't just simply answer him, but somehow came down and made the delivery Himself. Yes, this book is about miracles, angels, and prayer, and all three of them took place on that day because Jeff went boldly to the throne.

The writer of the book of Hebrews wrote in Hebrews 4:16, "Let us therefore come boldly to the throne of grace that we may obtain mercy and find grace to help in time of need." Do you have difficult situations in your life that you need help with today? God has a merciful heart and He's full of compassion. He's reaching out to you, asking you to come near to Him, with faith, just as Jeff did. Through His love and grace He will answer you.

"My thoughts are not your thoughts nor are your ways My ways," says the Lord. Isaiah 55:8

By 1982 I had fully recovered from my breakdown and I was back to my original self, taking my Bible everywhere that I went and witnessing, once again, on my job. But this time I was a stronger Christian because of the problems that I experienced. I have read that a pearl is formed as the result of a grain of sand that gets in an oyster's shell and irritates the oyster. A coating starts to form around the grain of sand until eventually a beautiful pearl develops. We have two choices when trouble comes into our life. We can grow angry and bitter when irritations enter our life or we can keep reaching out to God and seeking Him until we heal, just as that oyster becomes healed.

Eventually we will find that He has transformed us into one of His beautiful pearls.

I was now pretty much settled into my newfound church, going to college part time, raising my children and working full time as a truck driver for a building supply company. The yard foreman of that company was a young man who was about twenty two-years old and he hated me because I was a Christian. He would always make a negative remark to me about my faith or give me a hard time whenever we walked past each other.

One day as he approached me , he made some kind of sarcastic remark to me and by that time I had taken just about all the abuse that I could handle, from him. I reached out with my right hand, grabbed him by the throat, and picked him up in the air. I looked him in the face and said, "One day you will stand before God and then you will know that what I say about Christ is true." I had no idea that the Lord was using me to prophesy to him at the time. About three months later he became sick with what the doctors said was a rare blood disease. I realized years later, as I ministered to aids patients in India, that the rare blood disease that he had was Aids.

Not too long after that confrontation he died, and his brother died of aids as well, just before him. Before he died, I was in the front office picking up my delivery orders for the day, when he came in to visit the men there. He looked across the counter at me with an agonizing and knowing look on his face. I knew that he remembered what I said and I could tell that he wanted to talk. He was a walking skeleton because of the aids virus and I barely recognized him. The office was very busy that day, with office help and customers, so I was unable to talk to him. That was the last that I saw of him before he died.

The Lord had used me to speak to this young man. On my part, at the time when I grabbed him by the throat, it seemed like a moment of anger and frustration, but the Lord had a reason for it happening the way that it did. Maybe this was the only way that the Lord could reach him. What ever the reason was, it made him think, and I can only hope that at some time before his death he turned to the Lord.

Meeting Carole

In September of 1982 I was invited to a friend's house for dinner. I had not dated for over three years and I had no intention to do so. I was happy being single and raising my kids at the time. When I arrived at my friend's house I found out that it was a set-up. They had invited another friend of theirs whose husband had left her for another woman and their intentions were to get us together. Carole was a wonderful Christian woman and it wasn't long after we met that we went out on our first date. Eventually we fell madly in love and we still are madly in love to this day. After ten months of getting to know one another, comparing Christian values, and coming to the conclusion that we were equal in our beliefs, we were married on July 2,1983. We have been married thirty years as of July 2013. I have to say that the honeymoon has never ended and this is mainly because we have kept Christ close to our side.

Working with troubled teens

Shortly after we were married I took some time off from work to finish my last semester of college. After I finished college I took a job counseling in a boys' school for troubled teens who were from the streets of New York City and were sent there by the courts. I worked with them for about six years trying to help them and telling them about the Lord.

One day an eighteen year old boy who I had been working very close with fell into a rage and got into a fight with another boy. I felt confident that I could talk to ths boy and stop the fight. I made the mistake of approaching him from behind. He quickly turned on me, not realizing at the time that it was me, and started beating on me with his fists like a professional boxer. Although I was probably heavier than he was, he picked me up in the air and then threw me on the concrete floor.   He bruised three of my ribs, broke a bone in my foot, and dislocated my shoulder. I was out of work and on disability for a couple of months after that.

Only about two weeks after I was back to work another young man, who was twenty years old, perceived me as being an easy target because of the prior incident. He hit me in the head with a two by six board and put me back in the hospital. Later, when he was released from the school, he moved to an apartment seven miles from me and one day got in an argument with his landlady and killed her. As far as I know, he's now in prison.

Another young man who I was counseling was about sixteen years old. He confided in me that he had a handgun hidden in a radio at his grandmother's apartment. When I reported it to the social worker the social worker then reported the incident to the authorities and they found the gun and removed it. He also told the boy that I reported it to him. The boy was a gang leader and one day, after he was released, he tried to ambush me with his gang in order to kill me. Someone found out about this plan and I was warned. A police officer who I knew took my place and went to the area where I was supposed to be attacked. When the boys saw him they left and never bothered me again

Needless to say, the stress of the job wore on me and my nerves got so bad that I couldn't stand up to the anger that the kids harbored any longer. I finally was forced to quit my job because of the pressure.

My main goal while working there was to reach the kids with the love of Christ. My Bible was always on my desk and I was continually witnessing to the boys. The men who I worked with were always teasing me and would often tell me that I was wasting my time, and that I would never get through to these kids. But although they teased me, they respected me for what I was trying to do.

It began to appear that they might be right until one day a boy came to me and said "I want to do it." I knew what he meant but I asked, "Do what?" He said, "You know! Receive Christ!" I was elated. Six years of hard work and just one boy received Christ, but it was worth it. He knelt down on his knees and I led him to Christ. It had been so hard working with this boy and witnessing to him, but in the end it was so easy that I could hardly believe it.

But now it was time to move on to new ministry. I had been praying that the Lord would give me full-time ministry somewhere. I came home from work, two days before New Years of 1990, and told Carole, "Hon, I quit my job. I'm going to work for the Lord." I had no idea what that meant but I knew that it was time to step out in faith. Her response was simply, "Good!" The two of us had been praying for a long time and we both knew that it was the right thing to do even though neither of us knew what was ahead. But that decision was to take us into a world of ministry and miracles that we never expected.

Part three: Serving the Lord

Tithing and blessings

Until 1988 I had never tithed. During the first five years of our marriage Carole tried to get me to start tithing. Our finances were always in the red and it seemed that we continually had bills that we couldn't get caught up with. I told Carole that the Lord knew of our difficult financial situation and that He would want us to take care of our bills first. I had it so backwards. Then, one day as I was out for a walk praying, during the summer of 1988, I simply fell under the conviction that I should tithe. I have no idea why I felt convicted to tithe on that particular day, but I decided right then and there that we were going to tithe. The feeling came into my heart and it wouldn't leave.

Our finances have been in the black from that very time to this day. In fact the Lord eventually entered us into a ministry of giving our finances to the mission field for a period of ten years. As I look back on it, while writing this, the Lord was probably putting it in my heart to tithe so He could bless me in ministry. He couldn't trust me with His money until I trusted Him with mine.

Believe me, it's a blessing to dig down deep into your pockets and give to some Christian ministry that the Lord puts on you heart. As you give your last dime to Him and watch as He miraculously gives back, it builds your faith and confidence and strengthens your trust in Him.

There came a time in our ministry when we kept just enough money for our bills and gave all the rest, which was most of it because we had very few bills, to the Lord. Sometimes we gave the money that we had laid aside for our bills, to Him as well, when we saw an extra need, and He always gave it back. Our hearts were so full of love for the Lord, and for the needs that He brought to us, that we couldn't stop giving. The more we gave, the more He blessed. In Malachi 3:10 the Lord says to "Bring all the tithes into the storehouse that there may be food in My house and try Me now in this, says the Lord of hosts, if I will not open for you the windows of heaven and pour out for you such blessing that there will not be room enough to receive it." You can literally take that verse to the bank. Carole and I have tried Him and have found Him to be so faithful.

Going to work for the Lord

As I entered the year of 1990, I had no job but I had a whole lot of faith. I thank God that Carole's faith was strong and positive and we were able to stand together as we faced this new adventure in our lives. Carole was a high school Spanish teacher and we were able to live on her income that winter. I was also able to collect unemployment checks for a while because I had to leave my counseling job as the result of stress. It was difficult at first because we had her two daughters as well as my son and daughter to support. I spent most of my time praying. I didn't know just what I was going to do but I knew that the Lord had something for me in ministry.

By spring I decided that I would start a lawn maintenance business and use the money for ministry in some way or another. It was the Lord who put this thought in my mind and I knew to take one step at a time, to trust in Him and not worry about what was ahead because He would show up when the time was right. At the time I didn't know that the Lord was going to lead us into a full time financial ministry that would help support missionaries.

I already had a small pickup, a twenty-one inch push mower and a riding mower that I used around the house. I placed an ad in the newspaper, prayed, and sat down and waited. That first year I only cleared two thousand dollars and we helped support a teenager in Teen Missions with that money. That teenager was our very first missions project, even if it wasn't a large amount that we gave her. We still get letters from her and she now works full time for teen missions.

Business eventually got better and I added a dump truck, backhoe, bulldozer, tractor, various types of mowing equipment, and equipment for installing patios. Eventually I focused primarily on patios, sidewalks, and retaining walls and named the business "The Patio Guys." This name was eye catching and the business took off. We were always booked up and I ran the business for eighteen years, until I retired.

God blessed us financially in this business and as a

result we were able to go into ministry. It says in Isaiah that "Your light shall break forth like the morning, your healing shall spring forth speedily, and your righteousness shall go before you; the glory of the Lord shall be your rear guard. Then you shall call and the Lord will answer, you shall cry out and He will say, here I am." How true that verse is. God is so faithful. The light began to break forth as business picked up. He definitely was our rear guard and when we called on Him, He answered us.

As I began to understand what God's plan was for me in ministry and where He was sending me, I decided that I would work during the warmer seasons and send money overseas and go to the mission field in the winter. I also started a home butchering business for local deer hunters. I operated that business after the landscaping business ended in the fall. This always gave me work up until the winter months when I would go to the mission field and in later years I held healing services locally as well .

I prayed all year during that first year in business, for the Lord to reveal His purpose to me for my life. I always made it a habit to pray the first thing in the morning, from seven until nine, before going out on a job and we were never open on Sundays. On Sunday we went to church. I had a heavy burden for China and I prayed that the Lord would send me there. I even prepared a plan and presented my idea to the church one Sunday. I had a burning in my heart for the people of China and that was where I wanted to go.

Jesus said, in Matthew 13:45 and 46, that "The

85

kingdom of heaven is like a merchant seeking beautiful pearls, who, when he had found one pearl of great price, went and sold all that he had and bought it." Carole and I were after heavenly pearls.

Africa calls

Everyone that I knew was either going to West Africa or talking about the missionary work that was there. I was getting tired of hearing about the mission field in West Africa. I had heard of the need that there was to preach the gospel in China and that was where I wanted to go. Then, one day, my church showed a video about a missionary couple who were serving with CAMA Services in Burkina Faso, West Africa. CAMA Services is a world-wide Christian and Missionary Alliance relief program and this couple was in charge of the branch that was in Burkina Faso.

At the time that I saw the video, Burkina Faso was the third poorest country in the world. Tim and Ruth Albright were responsible for helping to teach the Bible to the people there and to help set up educational programs that would teach them how to develop a small business and how to earn a better income in order to support themselves. They periodically traveled through the country helping to keep all the other missionaries connected. They taught the Bible to the nationals and helped establish Bible schools. The Lord spoke directly to my heart as I watched the video and said, "You're going to visit that couple in Africa and minister there." Because the Albrights were in contact with all the missionaries there, this would give me an excellent opportunity to learn first hand, of how things worked in the mission field.

Again, I didn't ask the Lord any questions. I knew that He had spoken to me, just as I knew it was His voice when I saw the brass musical instrument before going to the missionary in Kentucky. Only this time I wasn't going to another state. I was going to another continent.

One thing that I do know is that when God speaks I move. If you want the Lord to speak to you and work in your life, first you have to be in a constant state of prayer and develop a deep relationship with Him and be willing to watch and wait. If you don't learn to watch and wait you may miss the opportunity that God has for you. At Gethsemane Jesus said to His disciples "Could you not watch one hour?" Two times He went back to them and two times they were sleeping. They weren't spiritually prepared when the soldiers came for Jesus. You have to be willing to communicate, watch, wait, and then move. Waiting is the hard part. Most people wait for a short time and then, after becoming impatient, they strike out on their own. There have been times when I've waited for years.

I had to pray and wait for a full year before going to Africa. First I sent a letter to Tim Albright and asked him if I could go and visit him. We didn't have e-mail in those days and it took time for letters to travel back and forth to Africa. Tim sent a letter back saying that I had to talk to his boss, Cliff Westergrin, whose office was in Colorado. I wrote to Cliff and called him on the phone several times. After a year of communication with him and Tim, I was given the approval to go. I'll never forget what Cliff said to me before I left for my first trip. He said "Remember, when you sit at the table with missionaries that you're dining with kings and queens."

Burkina Faso and the revolutionary war

I had no idea what I was getting into until I got to Burkina Faso. I had only flown once in my life and that was on a class trip to Spain with Carole when she was teaching. This trip was the real deal. It was definitely not going to be a tourist vacation. The airport at the capital city was unlike like any airport that I could have imagined. There were no comfortable waiting rooms or coffee shops with air-conditioned ramps leading to them. When I got off the plane in the hot African heat I had to walk down the stairs that they had rolled up to the plane. I then walked across the huge blacktop runway as the heat radiated up from it into my face. There was a large building in the distance where my luggage had been taken to be processed through customs. Soldiers with machine guns were on guard everywhere, watching us, as we walked off the plane. No one had warned me that the country was in the process of recuperating from a revolutionary war and that a new government had just taken over. Also, no one had warned me that the items in my luggage that some missionaries had requested were considered contraband and would most likely be confiscated and kept by the soldiers for their own use because of the extreme poverty that was in the country.

When I entered the building I saw a makeshift wall, about fifty feet in front of me. It was made up of army green blankets hanging from wires that were stretched from one side of the room to the other, and of course, more armed soldiers. Whatever lurked beyond the dark green blankets was a sinister mystery to me. I stood around wondering what I was to do and a soldier motioned for me to get in one of the lines. It was then that I realized that one line was for women and the other for men. Because I delayed in getting in line due to my lack of understanding I was last in place.

Finally it was my turn to step behind one of the army blankets and into the mystery that waited beyond. As I entered, I found myself in a small cubical that was also walled in by army green blankets. The cubical was about ten feet long and eight feet wide. On one side, there was a small table where I was ordered to place my carry-on luggage. It was to be searched by the soldier who was standing behind the table, who by the way, could not speak Eanglish. In fact, no personnel in the entire building could speak English.

Please notice that I said that I was ordered to put my bags on the table. There was no politeness here. Everyone was scrutinized, especially me since it so happened that all of my luggage was packed in army green duffle bags that I had bought at the Army Surplus store. Because of this I was watched even closer. The officer tried to tell me what to do but I couldn't understand him and this added to the confusion. Finally I realized that he was telling me to lay the contents of my luggage out on the table so he could inspect it. He watched me carefully and with suspicion as I shook with nervousness. After he finished tearing everything apart, he just stood there and stared at me for a while as if I were some sort of criminal. Finally he motioned for me to pack up my bags and go through the other curtain that was in front of me.

I packed my bags with shaking hands and stepped through the other blanket only to find myself at another table where another soldier motioned for me to show him my passport. He repeatedly asked me questions which I didn't understand. An African passenger, who was standing in front of me, decide to try to translate for me. This was a big mistake on his part.

The soldier asked what my occupation was. After all, I was carrying army duffle bags, which I hadn't thought of as a problem until now. I said that I was a landscaper, which he didn't seem to understand so I rephrased my statement and said that I was something like a farmer, and this caused more problems. Then I tried to explain by saying that I planted shrubs or trees. Now this soldier was looking at me with suspicion just as the first one did and my volunteer translator was getting very worried. He finally grabbed his luggage and took off leaving me there alone with my interrogator.

Finally, after being stared at for a long time, he told me to leave, out of frustration I suppose. By now I was the only passenger left in the building, and there, way across the room, leaning up against a concrete wall, were my two duffle bags, full of contraband. I walked over and leaned up against the wall as I stood next to my luggage. I looked across the room and saw yet another counter where I was to take my bags to be inspected by more uniformed soldiers.

I had no idea as to what to do. Because of the armed security, the missionaries who were to pick me up at the airport were unable to come into the building to help me. I leaned back against the wall and prayed, "Lord, help me. I don't know what to do. Please help me." I have never felt more alone. Suddenly, out of nowhere, an African man walked up to me. I have no idea how he got into the building past security. I only know that somehow the Lord had him come to me. He couldn't speak English so he motioned to me with his hands, are these your bags? I motioned, yes. He picked them up and took them over to the counter. The soldiers ordered me to open them and then this man spoke up. I don't know what he said but he motioned toward me a few times and then toward the bags a few times while waving his hands around. The soldiers looked at the bags and then at me and finally told me to take my bags and leave. As it turned out, this man was just a taxi cab driver who wanted to get a tip. God answers prayer, this I know. What a beginning for my first trip to the mission field overseas!

During the following years as I made trips back and

forth to West Africa, I took many items that the missionaries needed, because for one reason or another they were unable to purchase them there. I had taken American products such as cheese, chocolates, hand cream, and other items that the missionaries could not buy on the mission field, in my bags. You have no idea what it's like to have a desire for food that you're used to but have nowhere to buy it. On some trips my duffle bags were packed with electric drills, belt sanders, power saws, and of course Bibles. The Lord protected me on every trip. The soldiers never looked into my bags, not even once.

The Lord supplies the finances

One time, after I had just returned from a mission trip, a woman came up to me and asked how I managed to get the money to go on these trips. She could not see the spiritual because the physical got in her way and blocked her. She couldn't understand the miracles of God. I would usually go on a trip for about six weeks at a time and most people think that you need some kind of fund-raising program, or some kind of sponsorship and a covering by a church in order to do the Lord's work.

The answer that I give in response to a question like that is that my covering is Jesus Christ. The Lord told the disciples, as it is recorded in John 5, that "the harvest is ready but the workers are few." He said in Matthew 28:18 -19, "All authority has been give to Me in heaven and on earth. Go therefore and make disciples of all the nations," and in verse 20 He says, "teaching them all that I have commanded you," He has given me the authority so I believe Him, I trust Him, I take Him at His word, and I "go" wherever it is that He sends me. He says, "My sheep know My voice." When I know that it's His voice I go and I don't worry about the money.

The Lord has always supplied the finances in some way. Sometimes, when I leave in the spur of the moment, I put the money on my credit card and He always pays the credit card off in someway when I come back. I don't recommend that the reader does this without a lot of prayer. Don't go into debt and go off on some trip that you think you should be on because you were inspired by my experience or some other experience. It has to be based on your relationship with the Lord or you will fail.

This also does not mean that you don't have to belong to a church. All healthy Christians should be involved in a good Bible-believing church and tithing to that church whether that church supports them or not. The church is the body of Christ and we need to be lifting it up and we need it to lift us up. We can never stand alone. There may be some in that church who are doubters but it's our job to try to help them overcome their doubt. I've met many doubters who would have held me back if they could and it's only because of their own personal fears or jealousies. Sometimes we are forced to walk on a fine line of faith. We have to ask ourselves if we should trust the hearts of men or the Spirit who is in us, and we also need to ask if it is the Spirit who is speaking to our hearts or if it is our own desires that are motivating us. That's when we have to spend time on our knees before him. Ministry should never be about pride. If pride starts to get in the way, and it will, work on it until it's gone.

When I was taking my trips to Appalachia, I was attending the Nazarene church. Later, as I mentioned earlier, I joined the Christian and Missionary Alliance church and was with them for twenty-one years. It was there that I learned all about the missionary field and Africa. The church that I am now a part of is an interdenominational Pentecostal church and I have been with them for fourteen years. It was here that I met a man who introduced me to the mission field in India.

All of these churches stood by me and recognized my ministry because of my stable Christian testimony, but they never supported me nor did I ever feel the need to ask them for support, not that they wouldn't have, although they have sent finances overseas through me to give to the missionaries who were there.

I knew a woman who traveled all over the world to share her love for Christ. She never worried about finances, plane tickets, visas, or a place to stay. Somehow, in someway, the ticket or visa that she needed was always there, provided in some miraculous way by the Lord. She lived and served her Lord entirely on faith. She was not a licensed missionary nor was she sent by anyone. She just went as the Lord led her. Eventually she ministered in almost every country in the world, yet you most likely have never heard of her. She died while sharing the gospel in

Germany.

First John 5:14 says "Now this is the confidence that we have in Him, that if we ask anything according to His will, He hears us." In John 16:23 - 24 Jesus says, "I say to you that whatever you ask the Father in My Name He will give to you. Until now you have asked nothing in My Name. Ask and you will receive, that your joy may be full." Jesus was speaking to the disciples about ministry. I'm sure that this woman's joy was filled. I know that mine has been.

Prayer is a necessity

Since Tim Albright was with CAMA Services his work kept him connected with the C&MA missionaries who were all over Burkina Faso. I was able to travel with him for about a total of two hundred miles and meet the missionaries as well as many African leaders, and see the work that was being done and to also see the need that was there.

It became very clear to me after seeing the financial need there as to what my ministry would be. Over the next ten years the Lord had me travel to Africa, find various projects to finance, and go back home to earn the money that was so badly needed.

As I wrote earlier, I decided to work during the warmer seasons to earn money and send it to the missionaries whom I had met in Africa. Then periodically I traveled to Africa in the winter to find more projects while Carole stayed at home, taught school, and prayed.

A lot of prayer was needed and we were always praying, always in communication with the Lord. If you want to do any kind of ministry you need to pray. There is one thing that you will notice as I write about my experiences in ministry is that Carole and I never stopped praying. After we prayed we listened to hear His voice as He spoke into our lives and told us what to do. You need to learn to listen to the voice of the Lord and not listen to others when you know that He has given you a definite answer.

Many times people will attempt to project their fears onto you. Not to listen to others might seem like unsound advice but I've learned from experience that many people do not like to get out of their comfort zone. Don't misunderstand, there are times when the Lord gives us people to turn to. Just be careful not to listen to the wrong people and receive their fears.

Wells of living water

One of the projects that we liked to finance was wells that were needed very badly in this country that the desert was slowly taking over as it moved down from the north. Wells with fresh water were desperately needed and a hand-dug well cost around a thousand dollars at that time. That was a lot of money in a country that was struggling with poverty. A well that was dug in the right location could bring many people and would help Christians share the gospel with others..

As an example, in one situation, a large portion of people in a certain village where demons were worshiped had received Christ as their Savior. The unsaved villagers drove them out of the village because of their new belief, so they moved down the road a short distance and built a new village. They needed a well, so CAMA Services had one dug for them. Not long after, the wells in the old village dried up. The Christians who had been forced to start a new village invited the people to use their new well and as a result they were able to be a testimony to them. It reminds me of the story in Genesis chapter 40, how Joseph's brothers sold him into slavery and as a result Joseph eventually became Pharaoh's right-hand man. Joseph, later, told his brothers that they meant it for harm but that God had meant it for good.

There was one time when I was at home, trying to earn money to pay for a well. I had just saved one thousand dollars and was ready to send it to the mission field. The same week that I was about to send the money a man drove into the back of my landscape trailer at a high speed. He drove right up onto the back of the trailer as I was driving down the road, hit the tires of the tractor that was on it, bounced back off the trailer, and drove away. The force of the impact traveled forward into the drive train of my truck and damaged the transmission. The estimate to repair the transmission was a thousand dollars, exactly the same amount that I was about to send to Africa.

I knew that this was the work of Satan. Paul wrote in Romans 6:12 that, "we don't wrestle against flesh and blood but against principalities, against powers, against the rulers of the darkness of this age, against spiritual hosts of wickedness in the heavenly places."

I went home and prayed. I said, "Lord, I have one of two choices, and that is to send the thousand dollars to Africa or to pay for the truck repair." I said "Lord, you promise in Your word that you will provide if I trust in You. I choose to send the money to Africa and to trust You." That day I sent the money to Africa. It had taken me two months to save that money but because I made the decision to trust the Lord, He gave it back to me in one week even though I was unable to work because the truck was in the repair shop. That week customers sent one thousand dollars in deposits to me for future work. No one in their right mind would have told me to make the decision that I made on that day. Let me tell you, it's not about money or wells. It's about faith and developing a relationship with the Lord. If you want things to happen in your life, begin by working on your relationship with Him.

When I see something that needs to be done and I know that it is according to His will, I don't stop to think about it, I don't ask questions, I don't allow doubt to enter in, and I don't hesitate. I just do it. I have learned to move in complete abandoned faith and reliance on Christ. He has never, never, never, let me down. There have been so many times when well-meaning people have tried to intervene with their doubts and with their way of thinking in my life but whenever I have gone on a mission trip or felt that the

Lord was telling me to finance some project, He always paid the bill.

Our food should be to do His will

In John 4:34 Jesus told His disciples that "My food is to do the will of Him who sent Me." This should be the way we think as individuals and as the church, the body of Christ. We need to ask ourselves, do we think in this manner or do we think more about physical food as the disciples did in the fourth chapter of John?

If you read the fourth chapter of John, you will find that when Jesus went to Samaria and sat down by the well near Sychar that His disciples were hungry and had food on their mind. They left Jesus at the well and went into the town that was nearby to buy food, leaving John alone with Jesus to witness the conversation between Jesus and the woman who eventually came to the well. John is the only one who wrote about this account and he wrote it as if it were a first-hand experience for him. I believe that he was the only one who stayed with Jesus at this time. When the other disciples came back with food, Jesus made the statement, "I have food to eat of which you do not know." The disciples couldn't understand what He was talking about because they were thinking in the flesh and so they asked if anyone had brought Him food.

The problem with so many Christians today is that they have their eyes focused more on the physical than on the spiritual. Their physical needs get in the way of their spiritual vision just as it happened with the disciples and, as in the case of the disciples, many times God's will doesn't get done as it possibly could. But just remember, God always has an alternative route.

While the disciples went off to buy food, Jesus took the opportunity to tell the woman about the living water that He had. In return, she brought the people in the town to Him and He was able to minister to them. These were probably the same people who the disciples went to buy food from at the market place and yet they never told the people about Jesus, even though they were supposed to be close to Him. A miracle took place at that well on that day and only John experienced it because he stayed close to Jesus. There is a lesson in this account for us to learn from. If you want miracles in your life instead of reading about them then stay close to Jesus, otherwise you will be like the disciples and only read about what the other man experienced. Jesus told the disciples to lift their eyes and look at the fields for they are already white for harvest. We need to learn to lift our eyes.

Once, when I told one of my pastors of the burning that was in my heart to reach out to others to minister, I asked him if there was anything that I could do in the church. His response was that we had elders to do the ministry. We needed people to fill the pews and that I should sit in the congregation because they needed people in the pews.

After having that discussion with him I finally left

the church that I had been in for twenty-one years and found another church where there was more freedom for ministry. After only six months in that church I became involved in prison ministry and began to hold my own evangelistic and healing services.

Memories of Africa

Crocodiles, elephants, monkeys, cobras, vipers, and pythons are all a part of West Africa and Burkina Faso and I've seen them all as I traveled. I have visited villages where crocodiles were worshiped. The men would show off by going into the water and drag a crocodile out by its tail just to see our reaction.

Some villagers also offered sacrifices to large catfish that were six or seven feet long. I met a group of Americans while I was in Africa who had visited a village where there was catfish one time. They told me that the villagers took them to a lake to show them the catfish and when they got to the lake they were forced to take their shoes off and walk bare-foot through the blood of chickens that was poured out on the ground as a sacrifice. They were pretty scared at the time.

Once I saw a herd of wild elephants when I was out in the bush. When I approached them to take a picture, the larger elephants formed a circle around the smaller and younger ones in order to protect them. They looked fierce and very threatening as they flared their ears out wide in a menacing way in order to scare me off. It worked very well.

Another time a missionary and I were driving on a trail in a jeep when a large cobra rose up in front of us with its head swaying back and forth, ready to defend itself. The missionary drove the front tire onto it, pinning it to the ground. He gave me a tire iron and told me to kill it. Well, believe me, I did not get out of that jeep!

I've always visited in the winter, during the dry season when the country is brown and dusty. I'm sure that the vegetation is lush and green during the wet months, and beautiful to look at as well, but the mud is too deep at that time of year for travel. Rivers overflow and roads get washed out. In winter travel is easier.

People are everywhere even though you don't see them at times. When you're driving down the main roads, all you see are trees until you stop and walk just a few yards off the road and that's when you see the villages. Where there are people, there is sorrow, and a desperate loneliness for God. Sacrificial altars can be seen in the fields and cities with the blood of chickens and animals poured on them in the hope that their gods will hear them.

Mosques are in almost every village and the cry for Muslims to come for prayer is blasted throughout the towns and cities daily. Fetish houses are built of mud, usually just outside of the villages, and they are filled with fetishes where animists pay homage to the spirits that are in them. A fetish can be a charm, a mask, or even a vase that the witch-doctor puts a spirit inside of.

The country is a melting pot of people with a variety of beliefs, who are desperately looking for something that they can never seem to find because it can only be found in Jesus. Poverty is everywhere, Burkina Faso being about the third or fourth poorest country in the world.

Depressions in the ground that resemble a black pond can be seen from the road as you drive by. The ground is dug out and then filled with used motor oil that is dumped there by the trucking companies and then in turn the oil is collected and used by the people. Women stand ankle deep with bare feet, in the precious black liquid, dipping it out in buckets to be carried home and used as fuel or sold.

I think the children affected me the most. I carried a bag of hard candy with me at all times and as soon as I opened it I was always surrounded by many laughing, squealing, and sometimes fighting kids. One time I had so many around me, and they all started grabbing the candy out of my hands, that I was actually afraid for my safety. But mostly I had nothing but love and compassion for these children, many of which had illnesses and diseases, eye problems, stomachs that protruded because of parasites from polluted water, and most of all, the need to know the love of Jesus Christ.

I never saw factory-made toys in Africa. Every one was too poor. Boys would roll an old bicycle tire down the street, pushing it along with a stick, maybe running races with the others. Once I saw a little girl carrying the dirty head of a doll that was almost as large as her own, with no body attached to it. She probably found it in the garbage somewhere.

The boys were very creative at making cars out of tin cans. They would skillfully flatten the cans and cut and shape them to make the bodies of racing cars or motorcycles. They would bring them to the street and proudly show them off to me. It took them hours to make them and then they would try to sell them to tourists for a couple of pennies. The average income for a hard day's work was about one dollar.

I once saw a dump in the distance with people picking through it, looking for any scraps that they could find. When I walked up close to the dump there was absolutely nothing left but millions of small particles, not much bigger than a nickle, left behind by the previous dump pickers, and yet people were still picking through them, looking for a way to earn a penny. The people were very ingenious and they could take a worthless piece of paper or an old tin can and turn it into a creative object that would eventually sold to a passing tourist.

Large termite mounds that are as hard as rock can be seen throughout the country and once in a while a man in ragged clothes might be seen, working hard, trying to break one up with a pick in order to make stronger mud bricks. Mud bricks can be seen everywhere along the roads where they are made from the clay that is dug out of the ground and stacked nearby to dry in the hot sun to be used for personal construction or to be sold. Eventually they will be used for building the mud brick houses that are common in West Africa or the security walls that surround their homes in order to keep vandals out.

On one trip to Africa I met a young man who was a drummer and loved to go to the many villages that were scattered throughout the bush and share the love of Christ with his music. The people loved his music. While I was ministering with a missionary in the villages near where he lived, he traveled with us and I learned that he would walk for miles to the villages in order to play his drums because he didn't have any other form of transportation.

Just before I left for home I told him that I was going to give one of the missionaries some money to buy a new bicycle for him so he didn't have to walk as much. He told everyone in the village that I was buying him a bike and they all laughed and said that I would forget him. I gave a missionary the money to buy the bike before I came back to the States. One day after I was home I received a picture of him with his new bike and all the villagers were standing around him. He had a big smile on his face. Sometimes the Lord uses us as a testimony in the simple things. We just need to be faithful.

As I rode around with Tim, checking on missionaries, we would have to stop at various check points that were throughout the country and show our credentials. Sometimes there would only be two or three officers setting along the road and at other times we would have to stop at a station where there was a full police force. For me, being new to the country, it was sometimes a little scary.

I took about one hundred Bibles with me on one trip and gave them out to whoever would accept them and read them. There were few books to read in the country at that time so the people would read anything that they got their hands on, including a Bible, and read it from cover to cover. I found that the police were willing to read the Bibles while they sat waiting long hours for people to stop at the check points, so it gave me an excellent place to distribute them there.

One time we stopped at a station where there were several officers. I handed one officer a Bible while he was checking my credentials and he took it into the station. The next thing I knew I saw the captain coming out to talk to me and I thought that I was in trouble. He came over to my side of the car as I tried to conceal the bag of Bibles that were at my feet. He said that I could not give a Bible to just one of his men. If I was going to give them out I would have to give one to each of his men. To him, it was a complaint. To me, it was a blessing. Several men lined up to receive their Bibles and ultimately to read the gospel.

On my first trip to Africa, as we drove through the capitol of Burkina Faso, I noticed long lengths of iron pipe that were about three inches wide, all bent and twisted out of shape, sticking up out of the sidewalks. When I asked what they were I was told that they were the remains of bus stops and bicycle racks that were destroyed during the revolution when the mobs came past in masses and with such force that they just grabbed them and twisted them as if they were nothing.

One missionary told me that he had driven into town and parked his truck on the day of the rioting, unaware of what was about to take place. When he got out of his truck he noticed that the main street was empty. As he looked around he saw the police hiding in the surrounding buildings and waving frantically at him and motioning for him to leave the area. As he stood there, an angry crowd of thousands of people suddenly appeared up the street, marching toward him as they filled the street, tearing up anything that got in their way. He got back in his truck and left in a hurry.

Wood was a scarce commodity because of the large population. In order to buy or sell wood, a person had to have a special permit. The vehicle that you used to haul wood, whether a large truck or a small donkey cart, had to have black and white stripes painted on it in order to identify you as one who had a permit. As we drove down the highway we would see piles of wood stacked on the side, waiting to be bought by the dealers.

Handicapped people who were all crippled up with their legs bent up under them and using only their hands and arms to get around on, were everywhere. The doctors used an oil-based medication to fight off malaria, and if it was injected into the muscle in the hip by mistake it would cause the legs to shrivel up. Many opted to take the chance of getting malaria rather than to have the shot.

I once saw a handicapped man crossing a busy main street in one of the cities, on his hands, with cars and trucks rushing past him in both directions. A large tractor trailer drove up to him and stopped to block traffic so he could get across. If you ever have the desire to get involved in a project in Burkina Faso, they have wheelchair ministries for these people and a donation of three or four hundred dollars will provide a wheelchair for a man like this.

I was once invited to a village in the bush to have dinner at a chieftain's house. I was served donkey meat that was cut in chunks about the size of meat balls and breaded in ground millet. Millet is the typical seed that you might expect to find in a bag of bird seed but it is actually a grain that can be ground and used as you would wheat or rye. Both millet and maize, which is better known as corn in the U.S., are popular grains in Burkina Faso.

The donkey meat was so tender and delicious that my mouth still waters when I think about it. It was served to me with some kind of gravy over rice. Rice is another popular grain that the people enjoy.

Meat is scarce in Burkina Faso and animals are very seldom butchered, especially if there are other uses for them. This donkey would have been used for labor. I was later told by a missionary that it was probably either a very old donkey or that it may have been hit and killed on the highway, as many animals are in that country. Many times large tractor trailers with double trailers roar through the villages at high speeds and hit domestic animals that wander onto the road. Either way, it was still a tasty delicacy, especially in a country where everything that I ate was foreign to me.

Once in a while I would get the chance to help work on a project such as a new school or church, out in the bush country. Sometimes we would sit in the shade of one of the large mango trees that were everywhere, keeping out of the hot African sun as we took our break, sipping coffee and eating freshly baked French bread that was so popular with the nationals.

One day, while on such a break, where I had the chance to help work on a school that Carole and I were financing, I heard a lot of commotion behind me. Suddenly a chicken ran past me with some young men chasing after it, yelling and laughing. When I asked what they were doing, I was told that they were trying to catch the chicken for our evening dinner. Sure enough, at the end of the day, as we all sat around a big pot full of some sort of stew, there, sticking up out of the steaming liquid, was a chicken's claw. As I stared at that claw that seemed to reach out at me, the men laughed as one of them pulled it out to eat it. Nothing is wasted in a poor country.

The next day, as I was having my coffee and French bread, the same young men were running around, laughing, and chasing a dog. I asked, jokingly, if we were going to have the dog for dinner. As it turned out, they were just chasing it away from the cooking pots. Later, as we sat down to eat, they asked me if we ate dogs in America, because of the question that I had asked.

One time I was invited to have dinner at another

chieftain's house with a group of missionaries. This particular chief was giving us some land to build a church and school on, that Carole and I were going to finance. As we sat down in a circle in the yard beside the chief's mud hut, the missionary, who was sitting next to me, leaned over and whispered in my ear, "And you will eat." It didn't take me long to understand why he felt it necessary to make that statement to me.

A woman brought two large old, worn, discolored, coffee cans full of food and set them down in the middle of our group, which consisted of about fifteen men with dirty hands. Of course it was nice to know that their right hand was their "clean" hand since we all had to eat out of these cans, one at a time, with our hands.

One can had some kind of green slime in it that stretched about two feet in the air when you pulled it out. The other can had something that was brown and pasty-looking and when you put it to your mouth it had the aroma of something that someone had just dug out from between his dirty toes, that had been stuck there for two weeks before washing.

It was then that I understood the meaning of "And you will eat." After all of the fifteen or so men finished digging their, who knows how dirty, hands into the cans and digging out the brown pasty stuff and dipping it into the green slime, then came my turn. No spoons or forks were used. They simply didn't own any. I reached into one can and grabbed a handful of the brown stinky stuff, then I did as all the others did and dipped it into the green slimy stuff. I put it to my mouth and gagged as I smelled it and then swallowed it. I didn't ask for seconds as they passed it around again. I found out later that the green stuff was okra with hot pepper added and the brown stuff was ground millet that was cooked into a mush of some sort. If I had known it beforehand, it may have been a little easier for me to eat.

Even though I had some interesting experiences with unfamiliar food, I also experienced some very tasty African food. The women would cook maize, or corn, in a large pot over an open fire, into a sort of porridge that tasted something like oatmeal that had sugar on it, and we would have this for breakfast when we ate out in the bush. I think the sweet taste came from the corn. The main meal was usually white rice with either peanut butter that was thinned like gravy and poured on it or tomato sauce with fish or chicken added to it for flavor. Of course the fish head was usually in it or possibly some unsightly part of a chicken, such as the head or foot, but these meals were always tasty.

As I said, we always had fresh French bread and a hot cup of coffee in the morning before we started to work. The French bread was baked in outdoor ovens which seem to be just about everywhere. The bakers would cut galvanized, corrugated sheet metal that is used on roofs, into lengths that were about three feet long. Yes, I said galvanized. I can only imagine what it does to your health over a period of time. They would form the dough and lay it in the grooves of the corrugated roofing and then slide the sheet metal trays into large ovens that were made of clay. Because the

111

grooves were just about the same width as French bread the result would be a nice long, narrow loaf of French bread.

Nescafe was the only brand of coffee available and it was always instant coffee. So as a result you never asked for coffee. You always had a cup of Nescafe with your French bread, never coffee. Once we had our Nescafe and French bread, we would go to work while the women prepared breakfast in their outdoor kitchens and then we would eat about two hours later.

Once, on one of my trips, I stayed at a remote mission compound in the bush that was no longer being used. There was an interesting story that involved this mission compound which I learned sometime later from the African Christian who it involved.

One day I was introduced to this African man who was an elder in his church. He was almost completely blind at the time that I met him. He told me of how he had been imprisoned for being a Christian when he was young. He told me that the guards hated him because of his beliefs and every day they would take him out of the prison and go across the street to a field that was there and beat him. As he was on his face on the ground being beaten, he prayed over the land that he was on for the Lord to bless it. He did this every day until his release. The mission compound where I had stayed one night had eventually been built on the ground that this man was beaten on and had prayed over each day. As for the prison that had been across the street, it was completely gone with not even a trace of it's foundation left. The local villagers had carried every last piece of building material off to be used in their homes. The Lord had honored this man's prayers and his faith.

Another time, while I was attending an evening prayer service, I noticed that only children were attending the service. When I questioned the fact I was told that the parents were afraid to come to the prayer services because they would be ambushed in the dark while walking on the trail and beaten by the other villagers. They didn't bother the children. It was a strange and amazing experience to see only children at an evening prayer service. You would never see that here in the States.

Carole and I financed projects in Burkina Faso for about ten years. Giving of our finances was our ministry and this was the time period when the elders suggested that we put our finances into a retirement plan and go to the mission field after we retired. I'm so glad that we made the choice that we did. First of all, after Carole and I retired, we made one mission trip together and haven't made another one since that day. We were getting too old to make the trips and the Lord took us into a different ministry after we retired. As I wrote earlier, today we can testify that we are richly blessed in our retirement.

Never be afraid to step out to do the Lord's work. Carole and I financed a parsonage, churches that were also used for schools, a motorcycle for a pastor, bicycles, village wells, and other projects that I can't remember, as well as helping two African pastors to go through Bible College. This was the ministry that the Lord gave us to do all through the 1990's until 1999. In 1999 the Lord began to move us into a healing ministry as well as evangelism and our present prison ministry.

The power of intercessory prayer

There was one particular time when we were led by the Holy Spirit to have intercessory prayer together at our kitchen table. One day as we were sitting at the table praying, the ministry of intercessory prayer just sort of happened without us even thinking about it or deciding to do it. We started praying on that day and from then on things began to happen. It wasn't a planned ministry.

I think ministries that just come to you from the Lord, without you planning them are the best. This ministry, as well as the prayer table street ministry, the call to Africa and to India, as well as our ministry in healing and word of knowledge just came to us. As Paul also wrote, Jesus gives the ministries.

We took a piece of paper that day, folded it like a tent, wrote prayer requests on it whenever we received them, and set it in the middle of the table so we would be reminded to pray daily for the needs. Eventually the tent was full of requests both inside and out. The results of those prayers was tremendous. We saw relationships healed, people healed, finances improved, and so many more things done.

In Matthew 21 and in Mark 11 we read that Jesus cursed the fig tree and then walked away from it. In His mind it was a done deal and He didn't have to think about it anymore. He walked in a constant state of faith. He didn't see the tree wither. He didn't have to. He knew that the act was done. The next day He and His disciples walked past the tree and it was withered. But it hadn't been a done deal in their minds. They were surprised to see it withered. Jesus cursed the tree and had the faith to know that it was done, but they came back and discussed it. When we pray for something we need to walk away from it and forget it, knowing that it's in God's hands and He'll take care of it. If the problem reoccurs do the same thing over again. Eventually your faith will build and you'll see prayers answered more rapidly.

I'm not telling you that you shouldn't pray consistently. Jesus said over and over to be persistent. Remember the unfair judge in Luke chapter 18 who the woman went to for justice? She was persistent and finally he gave in. Jesus said to be persistent in prayer but He also said to believe. I'm just suggesting that you follow through with your faith. Luke wrote, in chapter 18:1 that "He spoke a parable to the disciples that men always ought to pray and not lose hope."

It's written in the third chapter of Acts that Peter saw a lame man begging at the temple gate. As he looked down at the man he told him to get up and walk and then he took hold of the man's hand and as the man stood up Peter led him into the temple as the man rejoiced over his healing. Peter knew through faith in

Christ, that this man would be healed, no questions asked. Then the people were all amazed at what Peter did, but Peter said I didn't do anything. It was done by faith in God through Jesus Christ.

I see so many people pray for healing for someone and then stand there and talk to the person about their ailments and sympathize with the sickness. At that point they've blocked the door to faith and stopped any chance of healing from taking place. We need to believe, as Jesus did, and walk on. This is the kind of trust that we had in Jesus when we had intercessory prayer.

There was a time when one couple in our church was angry with us because of a misunderstanding and it hurt us deeply. They refused to look at us or to speak to us. We didn't approach them or talk to anyone else about the problem and we didn't ask God to fix the situation the way that we saw it. We simply interceded on their behalf for two months and asked the Lord to bless them. That's all we prayed for, that they would be blessed. After two months of prayer they began to smile and talk with us and eventually they came to our house for dinner.

Prayer with faith and authority

Jesus said in Matthew 28:18-20 that "All authority has been given to Me in heaven and on earth. Go therefore, and make disciples of all nations, baptizing them in the name of the Father, and of the Son, and of the Holy Spirit, teaching them to observe all things that I have commanded you; and lo, I am with you always, even to the end of the age."

Mark also recorded this command in Mark 16:15-18 that Jesus said to "Go into all the world and preach the gospel to every creature. He who believes and is baptized will be saved; but he who does not believe will be condemned. And these signs will follow those who believe; in My name they will cast out demons; they will speak with new tongues; they will take up serpents; and if they drink anything deadly it will by no means harm them; they will lay hands on the sick and they will recover."

Please notice that Jesus said "These signs will follow those who believe." You and I are those who believe. He also said that He has all authority and He is giving us the authority to go. He said "Go, therefore!" It is also a commandment to us to go. If He has authority and commands us to go, then we should be able to go in faith, believing in what He says.

Fly trouble

One day, as Carole and I were praying, some flies that had gotten into the house began to annoy us. As we sat there praying neither of us said anything about the flies because we were so deep in prayer. The flies kept buzzing around my face and finally, while I was still deep in prayer, I yelled "Stop!" I said nothing more and kept on praying. In an instant, as quick as I yelled, they stopped and everything was quiet. When we finished praying, some time after, we looked around and saw that the flies had flown off to their places in the corners of the kitchen ceiling and stayed there without moving.

The incident reminded me of how Jesus calmed the storm in Mark 4:37- 41. It says that while He was asleep in the stern of the boat, a great windstorm arose. The disciples woke Him up and said, "Don't you care that we are perishing? Then He arose and rebuked the wind, and said to the sea, 'Peace, be still!' and the wind ceased and there was a great calm. But He said to them, why are you so fearful? How is it that you have no faith?"

One time a friend of ours had a dog that was infested with fleas. She told the fleas to leave and they did. I tore the ligaments in my arm and shoulder one year and was in terrible pain. I thought I was going to need an operation until one day, when I met a pastor who ministered in the gifts of the Spirit. He reached out and shook my hand and immediately discerned that I was in pain. He said "I sense pain in this arm and it will no longer be there." Instantly the pain was gone and it never returned.

In John 14:12 Jesus said "Most assuredly I say to you, he who believes in Me, the works that I do he will do also; and greater works than these he will do." If you're having fly trouble in any area of your life you can pray and trust Jesus. If you have let Him in the boat of life with you, then you can trust Him to change the circumstance around you. The flies will have to go to their corners and the seas will become still.

Forgiveness for my father and inner healing

One day, as I was sitting alone at the kitchen table engaged in intercessory prayer over the prayer requests that were written on the tent, I began praying for my father who had died many years earlier, when I was twenty. I don't believe in praying for the dead, and I stated this fact to the Lord as I prayed, yet I had this burning in my heart to pray for him. As it turned out, it was really the Holy Spirit putting the desire in my heart because I needed to receive inner healing by praying for him and getting a better understanding of what motivated him.

My father had been a hard man and very abusive to me. At some time in my life I had forgiven him for being so harsh with me. I knew that I had to forgive him because I was a Christian, but the hurt and the emotional scars still remained. Almost every night, at bedtime, I would remember how abusive he was and tell Carole how my life could have been better for me if he had been different.

As I prayed for him at the table that day, the Holy Spirit kept revealing to me, one at a time, all the hardships that had been in his life and why he had been so hard. The more I prayed, the more the Holy Spirit revealed the problems to me that were in his life and the more the Holy Spirit revealed his problems to me, the more the tears ran down my face until I was finally prayed out. My praying lasted for about one hour. When I finished praying I was completely healed in my spirit. From that day to this I have never felt the need to bring the past up again.

Jesus said that if we want the Father to hear and answer our prayers we have to have forgiveness in our hearts for others. The Holy Spirit will bring that forgiveness and inner healing to us if we let Him. Romans 8:27 says that "He, the Father, who searches the hearts, knows what the mind of the Spirit is, because He, the Holy Spirit, makes intercession for the saints."

The prayer table

One Sunday, a woman in our church announced that she had obtained permission to have a prayer table in front of a supermarket in the town near where we lived. She was unable to manage it and wondered if anyone would like to have the ministry. Carole and I volunteered immediately. We prayed all week that week before setting up the prayer table for the first time. Every Saturday morning we would set the table up with signs taped to it that asked "Can we pray for you?" Then we wrote all of the things that we could think of to pray about, on it. This was at a budget-type supermarket in a low income area.

We watched many people walk past us that summer who were hurting very badly in one way or another.

Every so often someone would stop to be prayed for. We gave out free Bibles, tracts, bumper stickers, witnessed to many, and led some to Christ.

All summer long, God answered our prayers. The people who we prayed for would come back the following week, and sometimes weeks later, to tell us how the Lord had answered our prayers by giving them a car that they needed for transportation, or a job, or a healing that someone in their family needed.

If you ever want to start a simple ministry, try opening up a prayer table somewhere in your community. If you are a praying person, God will answer your prayers. Just step out in faith and see what He will do. It's a great experience. Remember that James wrote, in the fourth chapter of James, that "If you draw near to God then He will draw near to you." There is no special formula except to have faith and to pray and trust in the Lord.

Angels in the field

One summer, around 1996, a local farmer gave me a tree to cut for fire-wood that had been blown down in a storm out in one of his fields. It was a hot summer day when I drove my dump truck out to the field and backed it up to the tree. I cut the tree up into sections that weighed from about fifty to eighty pounds apiece and started to load them onto the truck.

I always had a habit of over working myself and I was straining as I lifted some of the pieces. I remember when I lifted one heavy piece of wood, how I suddenly felt weak all over as I struggled to put it onto the tail-gate. As I put that heavy piece of wood on the back of the truck, I had the sensation that someone was standing behind me. I turned around and I saw, standing about twenty or thirty feet away from me, what I later estimated to be about twenty angels. They were standing in a half circle around me and they looked as if they had come to protect me.

They stood at attention like soldiers who were standing guard over me, about ten feet apart from each other. They were all just a little over six feet tall and they were holding some sort of weapon in their hands in front of them. The weapon was something like a sword but I'm not sure. I was so excited and full of emotion by them being there that I didn't take every detail in.

They all had long hair that fell just to their shoulders and it was neatly trimmed. I later searched the internet to find a color to describe their hair and the closest that I could find was natural medium ash blonde by Clairol. Each of the angels wore long trim white robes that were tailored to fit their tall, slim bodies and flowed down to their feet, just touching the ground. Their facial features and physique were like that of a tall, young man in his early twenties and in good physical condition. They did not have wings.

They said nothing as I stood there and looked at them. All of the area around them seemed to come alive in vibrant, brilliant colors. I could not believe what I was seeing. I looked around behind me, across the fields, to the road beyond and watched as a car passed by. Everything seemed normal in that direction, including the sound of the car. I thought that when I turned back toward the angels that they would be gone and it would all be just an illusion. But I was wrong. I turned back and they were still there. I stretched out my hand and reached forward, thinking that this mirage would go away, but it didn't. I stepped forward a couple of feet and they just stood there. I have no idea why I didn't say anything to them or why I didn't walk right up to them.

I cannot explain why I did what I did next. Maybe I just did not want to chase them away. I stepped back a few feet to the wood-pile, picked up my chainsaw and started cutting wood. As I looked up, they gradually began to fade away. It was as if they had been watching to see if I was all right and being satisfied, they left. I turned the chain-saw off and went and sat in the truck and cried.

I have always felt that they came to protect me from danger on that day because I was alone with no help. I believe that I was close to having a heart attack at that time when I became weak, because I had one a few months later and had to have three stents put in.

Demons?

One time while our children were still teenagers we

were having various family problems in our home. The elders of the church that we were attending at that time decided that our family was plagued by demons. Trusting their judgment, and not knowing what else to do, we began having deliverance sessions with them at the church. The sessions were extremely traumatic and hurtful to us and our children and I began having doubts that this was of God

Then one day they decided to have sessions at our house in order to get rid of the demons that we were supposed to have. As they were holding one session, our washing machine started running all by itself. They decided that demons were the cause and started casting them out. Later, I found that a faulty valve in the washing machine was the culprit and I replaced it.

After that occurrence we decided that there was something wrong with their ministry and we stopped the sessions. We got down on our needs and prayed and put our full trust in the Lord. In Revelation 3:20 Jesus said that "If anyone opens the door I will come in and dine with him and he with Me." I have discovered that Satan cannot dine at the same table with Jesus. When Carole and I began to get serious in prayer and invited Jesus into the situation our family troubles disappeared. After that we had harmony in our house.

There are many ministries regarding angels and demons today and I am very careful as to how I approach any of them. My trust is in the Lord. When Thomas doubted Jesus after the disciples told him that they saw Him, Thomas said that "I'll believe when I have seen his nail scared hands and touched the wound in His side." Once Thomas saw and touched Jesus He proclaimed, "My Lord and my God." That particular word "Lord" in Greek means supreme being over my life. Thomas saw Jesus as the one and only being over his life and so should we. We don't have to be concerned about demons bothering us or having to command angels in order to get things done if Jesus is Lord over our life. In Romans 8:37 Paul wrote that "In all these things we are more than conquerors through Him who loved us." I intend to keep my focus on Jesus through His word and prayer and on nothing else. Jesus said that many will come to Him and say, "Didn't we cast out demons in Your Name? And He will answer and say depart from Me because I never Knew you."

The revival

In 1998 some friends told me about a Pentecostal revival that was taking place in Canada and how the Holy Spirit was moving so strong there. I didn't want to hear anything about it because of the bad experience that I had with the Pentecostal church years earlier. They said that they had a video of the revival and they wanted to show it to me. I finally consented to see it in spite of my adverse feelings, and complained to my wife that I did not want to see it, as we drove to their house. I ranted and raved about how I didn't want anything to do with this movement.

We finally got to the house, after I caused Carole a

considerable amount of grief, and sat down to watch the video. After reluctantly watching a short segment of the video I knew that I had to go to Canada even though I was afraid that I might get hurt, as I had been hurt in Pentecostal churches in the past. I got excited and wanted to leave on that weekend, but it was easy for me to say because I was self-employed. As it turned out, I had to wait two months before they could take time off from work. They couldn't believe how quickly I changed my mind about going. When I looked back on that evening, I realized that it was the Holy Spirit who was prompting me to go.

Not only did I go with my friends and Carole that summer, but two weeks after I came home I went back, and a couple of months after that I went back again.

The friendship of the Holy Spirit

On my first night at the service there was an altar call for those who wanted to receive Christ for the first time and for those who wanted to experience more of the Holy Spirit. I went up front and stood in line but I was confused as to which line to stand in and I was nervous.

As I stood in line I talked to the Lord as I usually do and was asking Him what line I should be in. At that moment a woman who was on the prayer team walked up to me and told me to stop talking. Then, while in prayer, she reached out and touched my hand. I was immediately slain in the Spirit. Something similar to an electric charge went through my entire body and I was out , cold, in an instant.

The next thing that I knew I was lying on the floor with waves of love from the Holy Spirit buzzing through my body. They would start at my head and go all the way down to my feet, one electrifying wave after the other. There was so much love that I could hardly bear it. Later, I forced myself to get up and walked over to my friend to tell him how wonderful it was, as the tears ran down my face, and that he should experience it. He said, "Yes, yes, okay, Cliff," and that was all he said, so I just went back and laid down until it stopped.

One evening at another service, while I was standing with my arms reaching toward heaven during the worship service and crying out to God, something like a bolt of lightning hit the tips of my fingers and traveled all the way down to my toes and the power of God was all over me. I have no idea what it looked like to those around me but two women who were standing in front of me suddenly turned around and looked.

The power of God was very strong on me that evening and everything seemed to be going in slow motion. During the announcements I was still under the power of the Holy Spirit when someone on the platform started throwing free CDs out to the people. I was sitting about six or eight rows back when I saw one flying toward me. Because I was seeing everything in slow motion I just reached up and took it as if someone were handing it to me. I can still see the look on the faces of some people as they watched me.

Many people around us were falling under the power of the Holy Spirit and beginning to laugh, seemingly for no reason. Carole was questioning this phenomena until, one evening after the service, I fell under the presence of the Holy Spirit and began to laugh uncontrollably. It was then, after I experienced this touch of the Holy Spirit, that I realized that the laughter was a form of deep inner healing and when you laughed, all the pain and emotional hurts that had been inside were now gone. They say that laughter is good for the heart and it's safe to say that the Holy Spirit knows the heart. The scripture says that God is the discerner of the heart.

This was the reason that I kept going back to Canada. I just wanted more and more of this love that the Holy Spirit had for me. I couldn't get enough of it. As time went on, and I began to understand the reality of the Holy Spirit and Who He was more than I ever had before and I realized that I didn't have to go all the way to Canada in order to experience Him.

I began to search the scriptures in an effort to understand who this special Friend was. In the end a relationship developed between me and the Holy Spirit such as I never realized could exist and He kept drawing me closer and closer to Jesus Christ.

In John 14:16 Jesus says, "I will pray to the Father and He will give you another Helper, that He may abide with you forever."

Jesus said in John 15:26, "When the Helper comes, Whom I shall send to you from the Father, the Spirit of truth Who proceeds from the Father, He will testify of Me."

In John 16:13 -14 Jesus said that "When He, the Spirit of truth has come, He will guide you into all truth; for He will not speak on His own authority, but whatever He hears He will speak; and He will tell you things to come. He will glorify Me, for He will take of what is Mine and declare it to you."

After my experience in Canada I made two trips with my friends to revivals that we had heard of in the states. One was in Gulf Port, Mississippi and the other was in Atlanta, Georgia. These were both Baptist churches and the people were filled with the Holy Spirit.

While I was in Gulf Port, I had my first experience with the gift of interpretation of tongues. One of the worship leaders who was up on the platform spoke in tongues. As soon as she spoke, I saw in my mind an object passing quickly before me. It looked like a sheet of plain paper with two creases on it. It was folded like a letter that is folded and then opened up and placed on a table with the three folds rising up to the two creases. Two objects that looked something like long darning needles pierced each of the creases. They each passed through one crease and then the other. The complete picture was three folds pierced two times by the needles.

129

Then the words came to me, "three times hurt, two times pierced." It seemed to me that this was only a part of the interpretation and that someone else had the other part. There was a slight pause during the couple of seconds that I was trying to understand how to speak this interpretation when someone in the back began to read some scripture. I had no time to speak and the congregation accepted the scripture as the interpretation. Later I was told by a friend, the scripture was not the interpretation and that he perceived there was more than one interpreter. He confirmed my feelings, but this was my first time interpreting so I had become confused as to what to do

During one of the services in Atlanta many people received Christ, but one man went back to the altar after receiving the Lord and was slain under the power of the Holy Spirit. He fell on the floor and while he was lying there, someone stepped on him and broke his ribs. They prayed for him and seated him on the first row.

I decided to go up front and pray for him while he was there. My friend, Pete, in the meantime, had been told that I had broken my ribs. As I sat beside the injured man and prayed for him with my hand on his chest, Pete came up front and sat down beside me and put his left hand on my shoulder, thinking that I was injured. As the three of us prayed, Pete had his right hand extended toward heaven. At that moment something like a bolt of electricity hit him in the right hand, traveled through his body to my right shoulder and through my body and my left hand to the injured man.

Afterward Pete asked, "Did you feel that?" Yes, I sure did, and after that experience, and the one that I had in Canada, the Holy Spirit began to fall on people in the same electrifying manner when I prayed for them.

Ministering under the Spirit

As I began to walk even closer with the Lord, ministry took on a whole different meaning to me. I wanted to tell people more about Christ. I wanted to show them what He was willing to do for them if they would just put their full confidence in Him. Carole and I found the Pentecostal church that we are now attending and after we were there for a short while, I began inviting evangelists to come and speak. I rented a hall and asked an evangelist to hold a three-day conference there. The Holy Spirit moved in those services and He was beginning to move in me.

I eventually built a sound system, found worship teams to help me, rented halls, and held healing services of my own. People began to get healed and some received Christ. I began to move in the ministry of word of knowledge and discernment for inner healing, and as I prayed for people, the tears would stream down their faces as they received inner healing.

Word of knowledge and discernment are two of the gifts of the Holy Spirit that allow the evangelist to look into a person's inner-most being and see the hurts that need to be healed. It's a wonderful tool for helping people with. The Lord gave me a word for anyone who stood before me. It was a glorious feeling to work so close to the Lord, and of course, it still is.

This new ministry began in 1999 and it was that year that I also was introduced to the prison ministry that Carole and I are now in, through my church. I was invited to visit a county jail with one of our church members and sit in while he preached. He said he knew that I would be a little nervous and that I could just sit behind him and watch. At some time in the service he asked me to give a testimony. I got up and didn't sit back down. He ended up behind me as I started preaching for the first time in a jail. I fell in love with that ministry and have been preaching in jails and prison for the past 14 years now.

Carole's ministry

Before I go any further I would like to talk about Carole and her ministry. Carole always says that her ministry is to support me in mine and she has definitely supported me but she also has a ministry of her own. Carole and I were both in need of a loving Christian companion when we first met. Carole's first husband had left her for another woman. I don't think that either of us were looking for someone at the time but God had His plans.

It was only the Lord who brought us together and together our faith in Him has developed and grown, as well as the ministries that each of us have chosen or have been chosen for. We are both praying people, we both study His word, and we both seek after Him.

Carole is a retired high school Spanish teacher and one of her present ministries is volunteering as a Spanish teacher in the Christian school that is operated by our church. She has ministered at the local pregnancy center for about eleven years as a Christian counselor and has had the chance to reach the hearts of so many women in that ministry who need to know about the love of Christ as well as help save the lives of children who may have otherwise been aborted. She has been on one exciting trip to India with me and she speaks in the prisons with me as well.

Prison ministry

We minister to so many young men who have received sentences anywhere from twenty years to life for their crimes. Many of them have no families or visitors and when someone does visit, it's not very often. As a result, they look to us as a second mother or father and we get many testimonies of how we have touched their lives and how God has touched their lives through us.

We've seen many men come and go over the years. Some receive Christ, some become Christian leaders on the outside when they're released, and some even become pastors. There is one man that I know of right now who is being educated by the Assemblies of God

Church to be a pastor when he is released.

We are currently preaching to an average of one hundred and twenty men one Sunday a month. We preach mostly messages of salvation and encouragement in the Lord but on a couple of occasions I have held healing services. On one occasion a man stood on the prayer line and as I prayed for him he let out a loud groan and seemed to become weak. Some of the men helped him back to his seat. I asked him if he was alright and he said that when I prayed for him something happened to him and he couldn't stand up.

He had severe kidney problems and the doctor told him that he didn't have long to live. About two months later he testified in church that he had been completely healed. The next time that the doctors tested him, they found no problems with his kidneys so they stopped his medication. All the inmates were rejoicing and it was a great encouragement to them. I saw this man two years later and he was still doing well.

The greatest healing of all is when you see lives changed and anger and hatred are turned to love. Because Jesus comes into their hearts painful feelings turn to joy and happiness as a result of their salvation. Unfortunately there are very few volunteers who want to go into the prisons. People are fearful of what's on the other side of the walls. They are either afraid of the incarcerated or they are simply indifferent to them because of the crimes that they have committed.

Think of what life would be like for us if Jesus had been fearful of what was on the other side, on our side. He came out of the ivory palaces of heaven and into our dark and corrupt world. The writer of Hebrews wrote that He became a little lower than the angels for our sake. Just imagine, there was no Christ before Him. There was no redemption before Him for the world. There was only darkness for every nation on this planet. Only the Jewish nation of Israel had the sacred promise that would eventually be shared with all the world.

We like to hear stories about missionaries going to the mission field but at the same time we have a wide open mission field at our own front door. We have the sacred promise that Jesus Christ brought to us and we shouldn't be afraid to share it with others, even if it means going behind the walls of a prison. If any one who reads this book would like to learn how to develop a ministry, I will be more than glad to respond to your questions and to help in any way that I can.

Do You hear when I pray?

One day as I was standing in the kitchen praying I asked, "Lord, do you hear me when I pray?" As I stood there praying I thought, "when I sin the Lord sees it immediately" and then I thought, "If He sees my sin immediately then He hears my prayers immediately."

James wrote in chapter 5:16 -17 "to pray for one another that you may be healed. The effective prayer of a righteous man avails much. Elijah was a man with a nature like ours and he prayed earnestly." In Malachi 3:16 it says that "Those who feared the Lord spoke to one another and the Lord listened and heard them. So a book of remembrance was written before Him for those who fear the Lord and who meditate on His name." When I thought about those things, I realized that the Lord hears me when I pray. My faith was strengthened, that day in the kitchen, and I've never doubted that He hears me since then.

There was another time when I was taking a college Bible course on signs and wonders. This was just about the same time that I had begun to minister in the gifts of the Spirit. Each evening when we went to class, the professor would pray over us before teaching. She ministered in the word of knowledge and discernment, and I was afraid that I was going to get hurt somehow as I did earlier in the Pentecostal church.

Each evening I would walk our dog at ten o'clock for about an hour and pray. As I prayed I asked the Lord not to let her touch me, meaning, "don't let her hurt me." Later in the week, when I went back to class and stood in line as she prayed for us, she came up to me to lay hands on me. She suddenly pulled back and said, "Oh! I can't touch you. You're too hot." I knew then that God heard my every prayer whenever I went before Him.

Every now and then I think about that experience and I wonder why He would choose me. Why does He look at me? Why does He hear and answer my prayers? Why should He care so much about me? Don't misunderstand me. I know that all Christians have access to the throne but this is me, why me? I don't know. I honestly don't know but one thing I do know is that I have a wonderful Father who loves me.

I believe that this faith that I have in Him is why so many healings took place during the time that the Lord led me to hold healing services. I know without a doubt that the Lord hears me when I pray and He will hear you if you commit yourself to Him. There were many inner healings, back and knee injuries, and sicknesses that were healed in the services that I held. One man was unable to work because of an injury to his arm. I prayed for him and he went back to work. Later he testified that while he was working the pain came back so he stood there and prayed and repeated what I had said when I prayed for him and the pain went away and never returned.

Some times it would be something simple that someone needed healing for and other times there were more serious injuries. One evening a man came to me, in tears, who was completely deaf in one ear and was going deaf in the other one because it was injured in a car accident. I prayed for him and he went home that evening without receiving his healing. One week later I received a call from his wife to tell me that he had been healed. They came back to the next service and testified that when he was home, he thought that he was having a problem with his hearing aid and when he took it out of his ear to examine it, he realized that he could hear in both ears.

At one evening service a woman handed me an envelope with some money in it and said that her friend was in the hospital with diabetes and he wanted me to take the money and pray for him. I handed the envelope back to her and told her that I didn't receive money to pray for people. I told her to take the money back to him and that as she handed him the envelope she should say, "Jesus heals you." I received a phone call not long after saying that he was completely healed.

I held a few services at the Best Western Inn, and one day when I went to rent the hall, I was told that the staff had to clean the vomit up in the back of the hall after each of my previous services and it was too nauseating for them. They said I had to put buckets out if this was going to continue. When people have demons cast out, this is sometimes one of the after effects. People were getting delivered in my services and I never knew it. Yes, God hears me when I pray

Going to India

One day, as I was sitting at my desk, I received a call from a friend. When I asked him what he was doing, he replied, "I'm going to India; do you want to go?" Without hesitation I answered, "Yes!" I had no idea when he was going or how much it would cost. It really didn't matter how much it cost because I didn't have the money anyway. As it turned out, he was leaving in six weeks, which was in November, and by that time the Lord had worked out the money situation for me.

It was my first time to India and I went with a group of four other people. We ministered at an average of three services a day for two or three weeks. It was very tiring. There weren't any healings on that trip but we encouraged hundreds of people in the Lord and the Lord used the gifts of word of knowledge and discernment in me for the inner healing of those who I prayed for.

During the trip we broke up into teams. My friend, who was a pastor, ministered alone at times; his wife and another woman ministered together, and I was teamed up with the third woman, Barbara, who was in our group. Every now and then Barbara gives the testimony of how I was praying for a man, and as I laid hands on him he flew backwards, up against the wall under the power of the Holy Spirit. I was completely unaware of the fact and still can't remember it till this day but she continues to talk about it.

While I was there, an Indian evangelist came and spent three days with us as we ministered. During those three days he interpreted for me and we got to know one another a little. Sometime after I returned home I received a letter from him. He said that while he was interpreting for me, he felt that I was not able to minister as freely as the Lord would have me do. He invited me back to hold services with him. At about the same time an Indian missionary that my church supports asked me to join him in India for ministry as well. I decided to spend six weeks there and minister with both of them.

Healing in India

It was several weeks before I was supposed to go on my second trip and I wasn't sure of what message the Lord wanted me to share when I got there. I prayed every day for seven or eight weeks asking Him what I should preach. I wondered why the Lord wasn't giving me direction. I wondered why He wasn't giving me an answer. No matter how much I prayed and sought after Him I just couldn't seem to get an answer. Finally the day came in November when I was supposed to go to the airport. That morning I got up and began praying and asking the Lord why He wasn't answering me. Two hours before I was to leave for the airport to catch my flight, I was praying and the Lord said to me "You will do the work of Stephen. You will heal the sick."

In Acts 6 Luke wrote that there were complaints that the widows were being neglected in the daily distribution. So the twelve Apostles said that "It is not desirable that we should leave the word of God and serve tables. So they chose Stephen, a man full of faith and the Holy Spirit, and the others to serve. They set them before the Apostles and when they had prayed, they laid hands on them. And Stephen, full of faith and power did great wonders and signs among the people."

So when the Lord spoke to me and said that I would

do the work of Stephen I knew right away that I would be going simply as a humble servant but that great things would happen. Little did I know at the time how true that was or how powerful that ministry would be. It was on this second trip that I stepped out in faith, as I mentioned earlier and prayed for three hundred people for healing and then stepped back to see what God would do.

Again, as on my first trip, I ministered at least two times a day, but this time I was alone, with an Indian pastor assisting. The first evening I preached in a remote village, out in the bush, under a large, sprawling mango tree with it's ripe fruit hanging overhead. I used the moment to preach on the fruit of the Spirit and salvation as well as healing.

I prayed for at least one hundred people on my first night of preaching and many received Christ. As I was praying for people in the crowd, I laid hands on one young woman, prayed, and then moved on to the next. As I turned to the next person I heard a loud "crack" sound from behind me. The woman that I had just prayed for had been slain in the Spirit and fell on the hard ground, hitting her head. We knew that this was a real experience because these people had no understanding of what being slain in the Spirit was. I was concerned that she had been hurt but she smiled and said that she was fine.

I didn't realize until I stepped back that a man was lying at my feet with his head wrapped up in a piece of cloth. He said that he had been bitten by a scorpion and he was in great pain. I laid hands on him and began praying, determined that he would be healed. I prayed extensively and then asked if he felt better. He said "No." I prayed again in determination but the pastor who was with me didn't seem to have the same faith. He said that I should stop praying for him and pray for the others but I kept praying and finally the man was healed.

The following Sunday about three hundred people came to hear me preach. I decided to preach on faith in Christ and then pray for the sick. I don't believe that we should pray for healing just for the sake of healing itself. Healing should be accompanied in some way with preaching the gospel, otherwise it has no purpose and it's only an end to itself.

At the end of the message I had all three hundred people stand up and said that if anyone was sick or injured to place their hand on the area of their body that was injured while I prayed. I had never done anything like this before. I prayed for them and then shared a little about healing with them in order to give them time to adjust to any physical changes in their bodies. Then I asked that if anyone had been healed to please stand up and give their testimony.

That time in the service is when faith has to take over. Either you have it or you don't. It's the scariest time of your service when you have no idea what's going to happen. Any lawyer will tell you that if you don't know what your witness is going to say beforehand, don't ask the question. What if no one stands up? What if the testimony isn't what you want it to be? Will you look like a fool? You have to put all of the negative thoughts aside and just believe that the Lord has heard you and that the people have been healed. I asked the question and there was complete silence as three hundred people, including myself, waited for someone to respond. Then one person stood up and testified, then another, and another. Several people were healed on that day.

The pastor who I was with at the time didn't want me to have healing services because he believed that if the people didn't get healed they would go to the Hindus to be healed; but I held healing services anyway because I knew what the Lord had told me before the trip.

Finally, one day while I was in my room praying, I heard the pastor talking on the phone and yelling my name repeatedly to the person on the other end. When I went out to see what the commotion was about he told me that they were going to have a healing service and they were printing fliers with my name on it. I guess he was finally convinced.

The problem was that when we held the service I didn't preach on healing. The Lord put it on my heart to have a deliverance service instead. Many people were delivered from demonic oppression that night. Five families came back a week later to testify that their entire family had been delivered. Later, they built a church on the land where I preached. A few days later, when I saw the flier that was printed it didn't say healing services. Unknown to me and the pastor someone had changed the word healing to deliverance so the flier read deliverance service held by Cliff Montanye. This was just another one of God's miracles.

After ministering for three weeks with that pastor I flew north to minister with the evangelist who had asked me to come. He had no idea that the Lord had told me that I would hold healing services in India nor did he have any knowledge of the healing and deliverance that had taken place in the south. When I arrived to his town I found that he had a seven day conference planned and I was the main speaker. Hundreds of people came from all over. All day long several pastors took turns speaking each day and at the end of the day I held healing services. I was surrounded by Christian leaders who held doctorates and master's degrees in the Bible and I was humbled by their presence while , in fact, I was still working on my bachelors degree.

Many people were saved and baptized that week and many were healed. One deaf woman was prayed for and three days later she came back to give her testimony of being healed and how she was able to hear again. Someone else had a withered arm that was healed and others gave testimonies of various physical problems that were healed.

The Holy Spirit has always given me discernment whenever I ministered. I was asked to go to a pastor's house and pray for his family who was sick. When I entered the house and began praying for them I felt that the sickness was coming from beneath the floor. It seemed to be settling like a mist of some kind that was about three or four inches high above the entire floor and it seemed to me that it was demonic. I prayed against it and prayed for the family and left. After I had left I was told that the landlord had buried idols under the concrete floor in order to ward off spirits. It seems that this was the custom of Hindus.

People came to be prayed for by the hundreds. On one occasion a man who looked like a walking skeleton and was dying from Aids came for prayer. At another time a young girl brought her father to me in a wheel chair. He was a leper. Some of his fingers and toes and parts of his face were falling away from the disease. I've never been in situations like that before and it was pretty scary. I just grabbed each of them by the head and prayed for them. After all, what would Jesus do?

Opposition

Whenever a person enters into ministry he or she will eventually find out that opposition will come against them in one form or another. There will always be someone who says that you're doing it all wrong. It is always Satan's desire to destroy the work of the Lord and if you're the one who's doing the work, guess who's going to get hurt? People will either misunderstand your ministry or become jealous at some time or another and this can cause you a great deal of unnecessary pain, and why shouldn't they be expected to respond that way? People even questioned Jesus' ministry.

In Second Kings chapter 2 we read that Elisha followed Elijah right up until the time that Elijah was taken up to heaven in the fiery chariot. All the other prophets kept telling Elisha to stay back with them and watch but Elisha was persistent. He stepped forward and followed his heart. As a result, Elijah's mantle fell on Elisha and he received the blessing.

A friend of mine wanted to serve the Lord so badly in his church and yet, every time he attempted to get involved with ministry he met opposition from other members of the congregation. They complained that he was moving ahead too fast. They tried to get him to leave the church but he was too persistent for them. The truth was that they didn't want to get involved and he was embarrassing them. Many times, when people get stuck in a rut and have no desire to get out of it, they try to hold those back who are making an effort to climb out.

He pressed forward in spite of the opposition and got involved in the ministry that the Lord put before him. He eventually received a degree in the Bible through home study courses. He became a great influence in prison ministry, and eventually moved up to the position of assistant pastor in his church. He became the district director of a ministry that involved the leadership of several hundred men. All the time, as he advanced in ministry, the others were telling him that he needed to stop. They said that he was making them look bad. This minister of God was a praying man who was on his face before the Lord all the time.

Sometimes people get upset when you begin to step

out in faith, just as they did with my friend. Sometimes faith takes us down a narrow road that we have to walk alone on. Every saint of God has had to walk alone at one time or another.

One day a pastor that I met was ministering under the power of the Holy Spirit and he pointed to me and said, "They will say that you're of the Devil and you'll have a ministry to men." I didn't understand the prophecy at the time. He said everything in one sentence but they were actually two prophecies combined.

One Sunday evening, after a service at our church, some of the church leaders came to me and said that my ministry in the word of knowledge and the gift of discernment was demonic and that I would never minister in that church again. It was extremely hurtful and it broke my spirit for at least two years. It was my hope and desire that they would see the gifts that God had give me and use them in ministry at the church but instead they had become jealous.

At the moment that they spoke, I actually saw and felt a black object that looked like dark smoke in the form of a baseball bat hit me square in the forehead. It had the same feeling as if someone had actually hit me in the head with a bat. I believe that a dark spirit came against me at that time. For some time I was unable to minister in the gifts because of my broken spirit. I have never understood why it happened nor have I ever understood the phenomenon itself. I do know that Jesus said that He "will never leave you nor forsake you." Since that time my spiritual strength has returned and I am ministering in the gifts again.

Carole and I ministered in our church for five years before becoming full members. The day that we stood up front to become members my accusers sat a few rows in front of me. As I looked into their faces, the Lord gave me the discernment that at that moment they decided to leave the church. Eventually they left but the damage was done.

The first half of the prophecy that the pastor had spoken over me was completed: they had said that I was of the Devil. It wasn't long before our ministry in the prison began to develop. Carole and I eventually were given our own Sunday service in the prison. The second half of the pastor's prophecy came to pass and because of those two prophecies I know that I am where God wants me at this time in my life.

In the 26th chapter of Genesis we read that the Lord blessed Isaac with a great deal of wealth, so when the Philistines saw this they became envious and attempted to discourage him by stopping up his wells. Isaac kept digging other wells as the Philistines stopped the previous ones up until finally he was able to settle in one place. Abimelech told Isaac to "go away from us for you are much mightier than we are." The truth was that Isaac found favor with the Lord and it was the Lord who established Isaac. It may have looked like it was the Philistines who wanted the wells stopped up but the real culprit was Satan. As the wells are stopped up in my life, I intend to keep digging others.

Regrets that I have

I am sorry to say that there have also been times when I have heard the voice of Holy Spirit and did not listen to Him for one reason or another. There were times when I wasn't sure as to whether it was the Holy Spirit speaking or if it was my own thoughts and as a result I didn't act on the situation. Even though these are regrets that I have, they are still miracles in themselves that I missed the chance to experience and they should be mentioned here.

One day, after I had finished installing a patio for a customer, I decide to eat dinner at a local restaurant because Carole was away for a few days. I always leave a twenty percent tip for the waiter but on this particular day the Holy Spirit said "leave one hundred dollars as a tip." I couldn't believe it. I said "Lord, is this really you?" This would not have caused any inconvenience to me because I had fifteen crisp, one hundred dollar bills in my pocket that I had just received as final payment for the patio, and we had no shortage of finances. I could have easily placed one hundred dollars on the table and walked out.

It is not unusual for Carole and me to give someone a large sum of money as the Holy Spirit prompts us. We have done it many times. But on this particular occasion I questioned my thinking. For some reason I just couldn't let go of the money. As it turned out I had made the wrong decision.

Two months later, Carole and I were standing in

line at the restaurant and we noticed a plaque on the wall in memory of the waiter. It stated that he had been a wonderful man and that everyone loved him and he would be missed by all. He had been suffering from terminal cancer and he died shortly after the Holy Spirit had told me to give him the tip. I'll never forget that day. Maybe he was a Christian or maybe I could have led him to the Lord. I'll never know. Never be afraid to take a risk if you think the Holy Spirit is prompting you. He won't let you down.

Two weeks before I left on my last trip to India, the Holy Spirit warned me not to go because there were going to be severe problems and that I would never return to India again if I went. My wife, and a friend who was going with me, had spent their money on plane tickets and had spent a lot of time preparing for the trip so I was too timid to tell them that we weren't supposed to go.

We arrived in Chennai late in the afternoon and decided to stay in a hotel before traveling further to the north in the morning. Chennai is a very large city that is on the eastern coast of India on the Bay of Bengal. During the night two cyclones settled just off shore and created a huge storm with heavy rain and thunder and lightning all night long. The storm extended up and down the entire east coast.

When I went downstairs the next morning and looked out the door the streets were three to four feet deep in water. Travel was almost completely impossible. We found a taxi driver who was willing to attempt to take us to the train station. He drove through water that was half way up the door of the car. It leaked into the car until our feet were covered with water. I'm sure that the water had to be higher that the motor, but he drove through it so fast that he created a wake and the water went around us as it would with a motor boat and it didn't stall the car.

When we finally did get to the train station we waited all day long only to find that many trains had been derailed and swept over bridges. Buses were washed away as they attempted to travel the highways, and the airports were flooded. There was no way out of the city. We found a hotel near-by and stayed there. Finally, three or four days later the flood waters subsided some. Trains were still derailed but the airport opened back up and we managed to get a flight to the northwest where there was an airport open and then travel by car to our destination in the east.

We had many disagreements on that trip as well and the friend who was with me told everyone that I was old and dying. He even told my wife to get ready to live alone. I have no idea why he behaved in that manner, but it caused a lot of damage to my ministry there. When we came back to the states that friend called me to tell me that while we were in India he was chosen to go to the better places to preach while I was sent to the more undesirable ones. This caused me even more discouragement and as a result I never returned, just as the Holy Spirit had warned me.

We need to learn to listen to the Holy Spirit no matter what our own senses or circumstances tell us.

You can do it too

About forty years ago I met a professional motorcycle rider from my town who had become famous nationwide and whose picture was on the front cover of all the popular motorcycle racing magazines. He told me that when he began racing he didn't know anything about the sport. All he knew was that he loved to race. He didn't know that the motorcycle had to be maintained every so many hours. He just got on and rode, and he won. In the process he broke almost every bone in his body before he achieved his fame. As he raced, he learned, and eventually became the professional that he was.

In order for a Christian to do anything for the Lord, he or she has to have that same passionate love. We need to have a burning desire to tell people about the Savior whom we've met and then find a way to do it. We can't sit around and worry about the spiritual broken bones or the hurt that we may encounter along the way. We can't worry about the embarrassment that might come if we fail. We may not be one hundred percent sure of how we are going to do a particular ministry, but when we step out in faith the Lord will take the wheel.

Paul wrote that they were pressed beyond measure and even despaired for their lives at one time, but even so, he said that his passion was to preach the gospel no matter what.

One time our church decided to record the Sunday morning services and air them on a local TV station. The pastor asked for volunteers who would go every Sunday morning to show the video since it was a volunteer-run station. Six of us raised our hands to volunteer and we all went to the station to learn how to operate the equipment. When it came time to run the program I was the only one who went consistently. A couple of the others came for about three or four times and stopped. I ran the show early, every Sunday morning for five years, before our morning service until it was no longer needed.

Even the simplest work that is needed can turn into a ministry. God will use that ministry as a stepping stone in helping to build your faith. One of my earliest ministries was volunteering to mow our church lawn. There was a large piece of property around the church, and once a week I would take my riding mower over on my pickup to mow it. As I mowed I would pray for the church, and many times I would get off of the mower and kneel down beside it to pray. Not only was I doing a service for the church and for the Lord, but a type of prayer ministry evolved as well.

One year I met an evangelist who wanted to do some ministry in the county where I lived, so I invited her to come and minister in my area. I rented a large hall, I advertised, and I went on the radio on a live talk show to promote the ministry. I set up a three-day service and people came from miles around, including pastors. Many were blessed because of it. It cost me and Carole twenty-eight hundred dollars by the time we were done but it was worth it.

When I went to my pastor and asked if I could do the ministry under the church's name, he told me to take it to another church because he didn't want to be a part of it. I knew that this service was inspired by the Lord so I used the church's name anyway and as a result that evangelist ministered in our own church many times.

It was after this event that I built a sound system for three thousand dollars and held the services that I wrote about earlier, in local conference halls. People were healed and saved in those services. I think that one of the best memories that I have of those services was when one couple gave their hearts to Christ there, for the first time, and then came to our church for several years until they moved.

These are just a few more of the things that I've done in the past, and you can do it too.

Why?

I have not reached the heights or accomplished what many pastors and evangelists have accomplished and yet I have seen and experienced the wonders of Heaven that most men and women have only dreamed of.

At times the angels of heaven have come down and ministered to me. God's hand has reached out to me and touched me in so many ways throughout my life while, at the same time, Satan has tried to snuff out that very life.

Why? So many times I have asked why. Why has my life caused the heavenly realm to be shaken at times? Why should Satan be so upset over one single man that he would try to discourage that man so much and even try to end his life?

All of my life all that I ever wanted to do was to preach the gospel and encourage people to reach out to God, and I have, but not without struggles and opposition. I've had to struggle at times with the very people who I hoped to minister to.

Why? Even though the Lord has given me so many answers I still have so many questions. I probably will never know all of the answers until I stand face to face with my Savior and then the questions or the answers won't matter any longer.

I remember the story of the missionary who spent his entire life ministering in a foreign country, then, one day, it was time for him to come home. When, at last, he was home and stepped off the boat there was no one there to greet him, no one to say that he did a good job. He felt sad for a moment and then the Lord spoke to him and said, "But you're not home yet." For now, I will have to be satisfied with that answer.

One day, long ago, I read in Isaiah that the Lord asked, "Whom shall I send, and who will go for Us?" Isaiah answered, "Here am I! Send me." Isaiah was listening in as the Lord spoke and he made the decision to take a stand and live for the Lord. All I can say is that just as Isaiah stood before God, that I too, stood before Him and said, "Yes, Lord! Here am I. Send me."

No one has ever offered to send me and no one ever offered to ordain me, but God apparently saw a man whom He could trust. As I wrote this book I was reminded of all the men and women who have stepped forward in faith and changed the world around them. Jeremiah stepped forward and was imprisoned. Elijah stepped forward and was forced to hide. Elisha stepped forward and was rebuked by the other prophets. Daniel stepped forward and was thrown into the lions den. There are hundreds more who I could list. Satan tried to stop all of them but God blessed them.

In John 3:3 Jesus said, " Unless one is born again he cannot see the kingdom of God." and in John 3:5 He said, "Unless one is born of water and the Spirit he cannot enter the kingdom of God." When Jesus talked about seeing the kingdom of God He meant that we can see and enter it now, in the present. As I have written in this book, I have seen, I have entered, and I have experienced the kingdom of God and all of the miracles that go with it, because of faithfulness, obedience, and prayer, and you can experience His miracles as well. All you have to do is give up all that you are hanging onto in order to purchase the pearl of great price, as Jesus spoke about in Matthew 13:46. Are you willing? If you want to walk in the kingdom you have to pay the price.

I pray that as you have read this book that it has

encouraged you to trust in the Lord and that you will make the decision to step forward and let God make a difference in your life.

About the author

Cliff currently lives with his wife Carole in the town of Greenville near Port Jervis, NY. He and Carole turned 70 years old in 2013 and have seven children and thirteen grandchildren. They are both retired and are actively serving the Lord. Carole helps counsel new mothers at the local pregnancy center and also ministers once a month with Cliff at a near-by prison.

Cliff is presently writing another book titled, "False Doctrines; How will we know?" This book is designed to encourage Christians to study the Bible.

A third book is being considered with the title, "The Abomination of Desolation; Will we be ready?" This book is based on the great falling away that Paul wrote about in second Thessalonians chapter two and the two witnesses that John wrote about in Revelation chapter eleven.

Look for these books on Amazon.com: books, or ask for them at your local Christian bookstore.

Cliff on left with work crew and missionary in back next to a church and school that Cliff and Carole financed in Africa.

Nescafe and French bread under the mango tree.

Baking French bread in outdoor ovens

Congregation in a small village in the bush in Africa.

Missionary presenting the bike to the drummer.

Cliff with Pastor John and the pastor's
wife and two daughters in India.

This is a pastor we helped through Bible college in West Africa

This is another young pastor who contracted Aids before he became a Christian. He died a year after completing college and becoming a pastor.

Holding healing services in India.

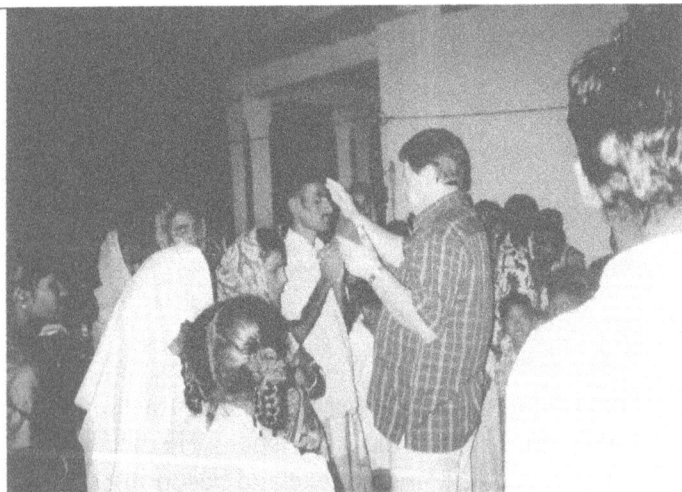

Praying for an Aids patient.

Cliff as a young boy about the age of
ten with his father and grandmother.

.

www.ingramcontent.com/pod-product-compliance
Lightning Source LLC
Chambersburg PA
CBHW060442040426
42331CB00043B/1088